WRITING
GORDON LIGHTFOOT

THE MAN, THE MUSIC,
AND THE WORLD IN 1972

DAVE BIDINI

MᶜCLELLAND & STEWART

Library and Archives Canada Cataloguing in Publication

Bidini, Dave
Writing Gordon Lightfoot : the man, the music,
and the world in 1972 / Dave Bidini.

ISBN 978-0-7710-1262-4

1. Mariposa Folk Festival (1972 : Toronto Island, Ont.). 2. Folk festivals – Ontario – Toronto – History. 3. Lightfoot, Gordon. 4. Folk musicians – Canada – Biography. 5. Folk music – Canada – History and criticism. I. Title.

ML38.T68M34 2011   780.79713541   C2011-902133-1

We acknowledge the financial support of the Government of Canada through the Book Publishing Industry Development Program and that of the Government of Ontario through the Ontario Media Development Corporation's Ontario Book Initiative. We further acknowledge the support of the Canada Council for the Arts and the Ontario Arts Council for our publishing program.

Published simultaneously in the United States of America by McClelland & Stewart Ltd., P.O. Box 1030, Plattsburgh, New York 12901

Library of Congress Control Number: 2011932377

Typeset in Perpetua by M&S, Toronto
Printed and bound in Canada

ANCIENT FOREST
FRIENDLY

This book was produced using ancient-forest friendly papers.

All photographs © 1972 Art Usherson, all rights reserved.
Gordon Lightfoot graphic © Morgan Narkiewicz

McClelland & Stewart Ltd.
75 Sherbourne Street
Toronto, Ontario
M5A 2P9
www.mcclelland.com

1 2 3 4 5   15 14 13 12 11

CONTENTS

"The waves turn the minutes to hours."

GORDON LIGHTFOOT,
"The Wreck of the Edmund Fitzgerald"

For my in-laws,
Mel and Norma

PROLOGUE

Hey, Gord. Or Gordon. Or Mr. Lightfoot. No, I'm going to call you Gord, and I hope that's okay. You don't know me, but I know you. We all know you. You're in our heads. You're in the walls of our hearts. Your melodies hang and swerve over the great open skies and soupy lakes and long highways and your lyrics are printed in old history and geography and humanities textbooks that get passed down from grade to grade to grade. When people say "Lightfoot," it's like saying "Muskoka" or "Gretzky" or "Trudeau." I dunno. "Lightfoot." Your name says as much as these things, maybe more.

Gord, I am writing this book even though you won't talk to me. It's a long story, but this is a long book, so here goes. You won't talk to me because of a song that my old band covered, a version of your nautical epic, "The Wreck of the Edmund Fitzgerald." Back in 1989, we contacted your late manager, Barry Harvey – a good guy; at least he was to us – to ask for approval, and he gave us his blessing. But then he said that he probably wouldn't play our version of the song for you. What he actually said was, "If I play it for him, it'll just piss him off." A few months later, something else happened, which is maybe the real reason why you won't talk to me. You see, after coming home from a tour of Ireland – an ill-fated tour; we broke up there, only to re-form and record your song, though you probably wish we'd stayed broken up – a music writer asked about our rendition. Because I was young and dumb and feeling disappointed that you – one of my heroes – refused to recognize our interpretation of what is surely one of Canada's most famous, and best, songs, I punked out. I told him that, "well, everyone knows that it's based on an old Irish melody. It's not his, not really." What I didn't tell the writer was that a guy in a bar in Cork had told me this, nor did I tell him that there were several beers involved – in Cork, Gord, this is a given. Later on, when Barry Harvey read what I'd said, he asked me to recant my statement. I might have just grunted and hung up the phone. Barry asked again and again, and, having grown a little older and less punked-out, I said I would, but then the story appeared on the Internet (the goddamned Internet). Barry was gentlemanly about the whole thing, but he said that I'd upset you, which is what I'd wanted to do, at least in the beginning, but not anymore. You were mad and I don't begrudge you that feeling. After all, the same guy who'd desecrated your song had called you a phony, even if he hadn't really meant it (Cork plus beer plus being rejected by one's hero plus an encounter with a drunken storyteller equals impetuous rant. It's a weak defence, I know, but it's all I've got). I tried taking the story down, then forgot about it. Barry called a third time, then a fourth time, asking nicely. Then he passed away. And now I am writing a book about you. And you won't talk to me.

Last year, when my publisher asked if I wanted to do this book, I explained the situation. He said, "Do it anyway," and so we proceeded to figure out a way to create a book without the contribution of its central figure, which is you. At first, I thought about using stories that other people had told about you, but the biographical holes were too great (turns out you're a bit of a mystery, Gord, although it's not like you don't know that). Then, as I started to look back through your life, I came across an event that I remembered reading about years ago in a Peter Goddard-edited seventies Toronto pop magazine called *Touch*. The event was Mariposa '72. Because it was a great event — maybe one of the most important in Canadian musical and cultural history — I was given a starting point from which to talk about your life, without actually talking to you. I also thought it might be a way of telling the story of Canada. But I tried not to think too much about it. Instead, I just sat down and started writing.

Gord, I know you know all of this, but, at this point, I should tell the readers a few things. Okay. Readers: the 1972 Mariposa Folk Festival (the sixteenth year of the event) was unlike any that came before it. It took place on a small isthmus at the bottom of Toronto, on Centre Island, now the site of a popular kids' amusement park. At the time, Mariposa was one of the most progressive festivals of its kind — only the Newport

Folk Festival and a similar event in Philadelphia had better reputations — bringing attention to marginalized folk, blues, and traditional music. It steered clear of emerging chart music — pop and rock and even folk-rock — instead scheduling time for forgotten blues masters, Inuit throat singers, and local tub-thumpers (Gord, I do not mean to disparage local folksingers by calling them "tub-thumpers," but it's kind of what they were. Still, I know that a lot of them are your friends, and I don't need to piss you off any more than you already are). In 1971, excitement over the event resulted in ticketless fans swimming across the harbour to get to the island, further dis-suading organizers from booking big-name talent for fear that the grassroots festival would lose its way. Such was their

Island ferry to Mariposa, 1972

monastic commitment to a toned-down event that, in 1972, evening performances were cancelled, in keeping with the philosophy established by artistic director Estelle Klein, who, in 1972, was out of the country, holidaying in Greece and taking a break from the festival.

By 1972, the music scene had changed. In Toronto, it had moved from Yorkville's coffee bar idyll to scabrous Yonge Street, with rock clubs being born every day alongside strip joints, pinball arcades, and gay taverns. These new places catered largely to the younger music fan, blessed by the drinking age in Ontario having been lowered, a year earlier, from twenty-one to eighteen. Also, because of 1971 federal legislation that required radio stations to play 33⅓ per cent Canadian music, the nation's sonic palette widened and there was room for new bands driven by fuzz-toned guitarists and wild-haired singers who felt empowered after hearing themselves on the radio for the first time. The city's musical culture moulted. New sounds were being heard everywhere. Everywhere, that is, except at the largest and most stubborn-minded music festival in Canada.

When Mariposa organizers sat down to program the playbill for that year's festival, they pencilled in Murray McLauchlan and Bruce Cockburn as the de facto headliners. Gord, I'm sure that you would have headlined the festival had you not been suffering through your shittiest year ever. By '72, you'd stopped touring, and you were dating Cathy Evelyn Smith, the same woman who'd conceived Levon Helm's love child in the Seahorse Inn on Toronto's southern Etobicoke lakeshore and who was later charged with murder in the speedball death of John Belushi. You had also suffered the first symptoms of Bell's palsy during a performance at Massey Hall and, in 1971, had waged a trying battle with Grammy organizers, who demanded that you shorten "If You Could Read My Mind." Anyway, because of your stasis, the responsibility for headlining the bill fell to two of your Yorkville proteges, both of whom, because of the new CanCon rules, had usurped a musical territory that, before the new law, had been almost exclusively yours. I don't know if that cheesed you, Gord. I don't even know whether, because you were lost in a deep fog of booze and drugs and pain, any of this registered. Maybe it did. It's one of the things I hope to figure out.

Anyway, what happened on that island that weekend was an unexpected confluence of the greatest songwriters of their age, each of them – like yourself – emerging from difficult times. That it happened in my city – in your city, in our city – puts me close to the memory, although I would have been way too young to go there myself. Because it's one of these great events that hasn't been written about, I couldn't pass up the opportunity. Writers live for this sort of thing: an untold story. The same could be said for you, Gord. It's been over thirty years since anyone wrote a book about you. It is time.

Still, the ideas didn't end there. After poring over newsprint and microfilm about Mariposa '72 at the Toronto Reference Library and other places, I found that the story grew and grew. What I learned was that, over the seven days leading up to Mariposa, there occurred some of the era's most memorable and profound moments in music, politics, sports, and culture, both at home and abroad. What happened from July 10 to July 17 eclipsed any single story, including your own. In Canada, the Canada–Russia hockey teams were announced; the largest jailbreak in Canadian history occurred at Kingston's Millhaven penitentiary; and, through a combination of forces, Trudeaumania fell fast and hard. The summer of 1972 was also when The Rolling Stones staged one of the most important – and notorious – rock and roll tours ever, in support of their important and notorious album, *Exile on Main Street*. As it turns out, they were also in Toronto during the Mariposa weekend, playing two shows at Maple Leaf Gardens. Stevie Wonder opened and filmmaker Robert Frank and writer Truman Capote were in tow. On Sunday in Montreal, their equipment truck was bombed in a loading bay behind the Forum. Some said the separatists were responsible, but no one knows for sure.

World news of that week is also filled with remarkable events large and small, including the beginning of the Bobby Fischer–Boris Spassky chess summit and the journey of Pioneer 10 towards Jupiter. The week started with a total eclipse of the sun, and when the bells rang out on the evening of December 31, 1972, they ended the longest twelve months in history – three seconds having been added to international time – and something about music, something about Canada, and something about the world was different than it had been before.

Gord, before I started writing, I talked to people who know you. I was given advice on how to handle the situation, which proved to be no advice at all. When I announced my intentions, some folks told me to steer clear. "Whatever you do, don't park outside his house," said one person. "The last guy who did this had his car pissed on by him. He's a grumpy old man. He'll never talk to you." Others were more encouraging. "Gord is a beautiful person," said Dan Hill. "After Paul [Quarrington] died, he really helped me get through my period of grieving." Eventually, I was left with two impressions. From what I gathered, you were either a loner or you were everybody's good time. You were either a tough guy or a sweetheart who could break down at a moment's notice. You were either a shit-kicking cowboy or an angel; a drunk or a saint. You'd either steal someone's girlfriend or give him the shirt off your back. You were either Canada's Townes Van Zandt or a Roger Whittaker wannabe in a plaid shirt. You were either hell on your band or loyal to a fault. You either loved Canada or had tried as hard as you could to get the hell out. Your small-town roots were either the driving force of your art, or the small, airless pepper box in which your life was confined. You were either here – showing up at LeafsP games or attending industry banquets – or not here – disappearing to go on long canoe trips, or hiding out in a friend's apartment in Detroit.

Because you won't talk to me – I've called your record company a bunch of times, written emails, all of that, and still nothing – I decided to write you a letter, which, by now, is kind of obvious. I should also tell you that this book alternates between a letter to you and a description of the events of that week in '72, leading up to Mariposa and a wild prose crescendo that will leave even the crustiest old critic lachrymose and braying from his knees.

There's one other thing, Gord. It's actually a big thing. You see, in the letter sections, I've made stuff up. Some of it might have happened; some of it might not. Because you won't talk to me, I'm left having to imagine your life. Because I'm a musician, too, I wanted to use all that I've seen and heard and done in my own rock and roll life to help piece together your story; to understand how you – a small-town choirboy – ended up creating this country's most formidable body of song. The lawyers don't want me to write this book, Gord. They think you will come and find me and drag this book down. My wife doesn't want me to write it. She doesn't want our car pissed on. But no artist ever did anything based on whether a lawyer liked their idea or not. Well, maybe some did, but not me. Still, if you won't talk to me, Gord, I'm going to talk to you. I mean, it wouldn't be the first conversation that started without both people listening.

So, okay, Gord.

I'll start.

'72

MONDAY, JULY 10TH

On Monday afternoon at 3:21, they walked outside holding tinfoil periscopes, kleenex dispensers, and cigar boxes polka-dotted with holes. A child lifted an empty bandage box with an opening slivered at one end, its contents spilled at his ankles, while he stood on a hill waiting for the world to swallow itself. Handfuls of others eschewed such crude devices, glued and taped at kitchen tables and work benches, choosing, instead, to simply tent their fingers above their brows as they stared bravely, foolishly, at the sun, which, a few hours past the North American midday in the slow molasses of a moment, would disappear completely. The lighted world would darken save for a band of gold which played at the edges of the moon — the new moon — before the eclipse held in the sky like a celestial motorist pausing to look down at everyone else looking up. Their eyes counted the seconds. The world was pressed into a single motionless black shape.

———

Darkness grew in other parts of the world, too; places like Orissa, in Northeastern India, where, on Monday, the Kabari tradesman Abdi Sultam lay on a bamboo mat in his wooden hut waiting for the eclipse to cool the scorched grounds of his small Gadjat village. Abdi's settlement had been carved by his ancestors out of the Chandaka forest, home to chitals, barking deer, wild pigs, rhesus monkeys, rudder mongoose, crested serpent eagles, pangolins, Indian wolves, rock pythons, Bengal lizards, and, most famously, the world's largest elephant reserve. Nineteen seventy-two had produced a mercilessly hot summer, and drought had robbed villagers and surrounding wildlife of their most basic needs, which is why Abdi was hoping that the day's celestial event might work to relieve the torpor of the season. As time lengthened, he sensed the shadows swelling above him, and the fringes of the sky growing dim as the moon cruised towards its white-hot target. Abdi placed a sabatari leaf on his tongue, crossed his arms over his chest, and closed his eyes. Soon, top and bottom, up and down, north and south, and past and future folded together, and anything that wasn't rooted deep into the earth dimmed as if it had been tipped into a pot of black ink. If this darkness was comforting to Abdi, it created terror in the forest's beasts, especially the elephants, who had also suffered through the heat and drought, but for whom the eclipse was no reprieve. Instead, the sky's sudden darkness was like the final gesture of a great and terrifying power. Abdi heard the footfalls of the enormous beasts, and thought nothing of it, not at first. But the sound grew louder, the footfalls more hurried and stressed: the elephants were going crazy. The light of the day eventually returned, but by the time Monday descended into Tuesday, twenty-four villagers had been trampled to death. The Chandaka settlements were left in tatters.

The eclipse was visible in Atlantic Canada, but nowhere else in the country. In Southern Ontario, clouds as thick as gauze rolled in from the lake, making the Kingston shoreline dark and grim for most of the day. Still, the warden at Millhaven, the new maximum security prison, kept the prisoners inside. In the late afternoon, the men were let out to play softball; something about prisoners' rights, and recreation and exercise, too. The field had been a bone of contention among the community when it was first built, as it was superior to many of the county's diamonds, fitted with lights and groomed base paths and a new unblemished dish for home plate. The convicts called their team the Sabres; or rather, it's what the warden allowed it to be called. A team sponsored by a local hotel – the Portsmouth House Petes – provided the day's opposition, although some people wondered why anyone would voluntarily step past the barbed wire fences into the compound. And if softball was considered a peaceful game by prison organizers, this assumption was largely lost on the inmates. To them, a bat wasn't a plaything, at least not when held by someone like Donald Oag, who'd killed two inmates during the Kingston Pen riots of '71, and whose face had been bludgeoned flat by sadness and anger after a lifetime spent around shitty people and worse parents. To him, and others like him, holding the bat evoked the sensation of swinging a heavy wooden plank onto a small amphibian too slow and dim-witted to move; or how the tire iron sounded as it landed on the thug's back, whom he hit harder then hit some more. Oag hated his life and had tried to kill himself several times while in custody. He was a mean and tortured man, if not without complications. During his KP trial, guards testified that if it hadn't been for Oag's actions – subduing and ultimately killing two inmates hell-bent on taking the guards down with them – they never would have survived the ordeal. Whether it was an act of mercy was beside the point.

The psychiatrists and doctors employed by Millhaven ex-plained to the warden that playing baseball was about tension release, or transference of rage, or some other bullshit, thought the warden, because, really, you'd have to be the dumbest rube alive to believe that any of that would work on these hard cases. If anything came from the game, it would be that the inmates and the guards might, if only for a few seconds, forget the misery of their circumstance, because only a few feet of metal fence separated those who slept behind bars at night and those who, at the end of the day, were able to go home in freedom to their wives and family, which some suggested was no freedom at all.

In 1972 America, freedom was a go-to word. It was a silver belt-buckle, a red-white-and-blue bumper sticker, and countless slogans for infinite products: Ride the Free Skies, The Freedom Trail, The Taste of Freedom, Freedom's Just Another Word for the Music of Kris Kristofferson and Janis Joplin. People lived in the free-to-be-you-and-me world of Dick Allen and Evel Knievel, Woodward and Bernstein. Freedom was enormous cars for everyone, fast food that didn't kill you (not yet), gleaming new liquor stores selling beer and spirits in integrated neighbourhoods, *The Happy Hooker*, Grand Funk Railroad, key parties, cigarettes that made you tall and handsome and popular (and didn't kill you; not yet), and slow-mo colour-drenched NFL films broadcast on TV stations that started with either *w* or *k*. In 1972, freedom was also about space, or rather, space travel, and while most Americans spent the early hours of July 10 staring at the sky looking for the eclipse, there were a few dozen who looked deeper at a tiny spacecraft scuttling farther into the galaxy than anything that had come before it.

NASA called it Pioneer 10, although its name was based on blind hope as much as anything. The purpose of the spacecraft was to travel past Mars into Jupiter's asteroid belt, becoming the first artificial object to leave the solar system. The odds were uninspiring. Pioneer 10 was launched on the morning of March 2, 1972, from Complex 36A Cape Canaveral, and sometime in June, it crossed the orbit of Mars. On July 10, MIT and UCLA bioengineers, mathematicians, physicists, and aeronautic architects wearing starched white shirts with pocket protectors sat staring at a *Dr. Strangelove* tracking screen, smoking cigarettes and drinking sweetened coffee from styrofoam cups, waiting to see if the spacecraft would maintain its trajectory and move through the asteroid belt, avoiding rocks both office-chair small and Alaska-huge, moving at fearsome speeds, something that no spacecraft had ever done before. A few days passed, so they waited a little bit longer. More coffee.

On Monday, organizers of the Mariposa Folk Festival sat in their offices staring at the schematic of that weekend's lineup: who would play where and when and with whom. Mariposa was first conceived in 1961, in Orillia – a hamlet on the shores of Lake Simcoe – and named after the fictional town in Stephen Leacock's enduring classic, *Sunshine Sketches of a Little Town*. Since its beginning, every year had been different, but the 1971 event had been different in a new way. That weekend, the festival lost $4,000 amid conflicts caused by sixties hold-over fans who feared that the festival was getting too big, and who protested increased ticket prices and an emphasis on name acts to carry the weight. Staring at the performance grid, the organizers measured the acts on paper, and to them, things looked alright. There was lots of traditional blues – Roosevelt Sykes and Bukka White – as well as banjo workshops, Newfie songs and stories, the great country duo Hazel and Alice, and the Mississippi Fife and Drum group. Along with newcomers McLauchlan and Cockburn, Bonnie Raitt, playing for the first time in Canada, was booked, as was John Prine, who'd been

Bonnie Raitt at Mariposa, 1972

discovered by Kris Kristofferson and was managed by Paul Anka. Drawing a box around these performances, the men and women – who were sitting for the first time without their artistic director, den mother, and guiding light, Estelle Klein – rested their pens on the table feeling confident that the festival would go off as planned, without any unforeseen complications. There would be no stars, no surprises. They waited for Friday.

Roger Begin ached for Friday. No. He ached for Tuesday. No. He ached for tomorrow. Long-haired and free-spirited – probably rainbow-bandanaed, too – Roger spent his Monday evening lying torched on the cool sheets of a hospital bed in Ottawa. The previous day, Sunday, had been a very bad day, the worst of his life. It had started out fine, exhilarating even. Jumping for the first time under the guidance of the Sports Ontario Skydiving School, the nineteen-year-old had partly quavered with fear, partly tried not to vomit, and partly imagined himself standing at God's shoulder while waiting at the lip of the plane's door, which a man in goggles had thrown open for him. Roger tried looking for his parents standing in the fields below, but he'd lost them in the land's vast and magnificent quilt work, which lay 2,500 feet below. The goggled man counted to ten and then, bravely, inexcusably, and perhaps foolishly, Roger leapt.

Somewhere within that Central Ontario quilt work, Jennifer Mitchell, eighteen, let herself become swallowed by her beanbag chair as she turned the album over and over in her hands, headphones the size of enormous clams strapped to her sandy-blond hair. She hadn't listened to Dylan for awhile, and for the first time, his music sounded kind of old, even though he was still, unquestionably, the greatest poet of his generation. The vinyl had been played to death, too: popping and crackling and *grzzzzing* as the needle with the penny taped to it dragged itself across side one, then side two, which she heralded by smoking a roach that she'd found poking out from the edge of the Persian rug given to her by an old boyfriend who'd brought it home after a trip to Marrakesh. Dylan hadn't been seen or heard from lately – he hadn't put out a new record in a while, either – and for a moment, Jenn wondered whether or not she was growing nostalgic at eighteen, a notion that frightened and appalled her, edging too close, she worried, to becoming like one of the Old Persons, under whose rules she suffered every day. Reaching from her chair while trying to move as little as possible, she flung the tone arm from *Highway 61 Revisited,* frisbeed the record into her vinyl pile, and pancaked Led Zeppelin onto the turntable's rubber mat. Electric guitars, yeah. "Dazed and Confused" made her wonder why she'd ever said she'd go to Mariposa, but at least Terry and Janice would be there. At least it was a weekend away from the Old Persons, and that wouldn't be all bad.

Meanwhile, Roger fell. The sky opened all robin's egg blue and he moved through it, the wind screaming as the plane cruised away. He'd been taught to manoeuvre the controls on the parachute just so, and because he was relatively close to the ground it would have been easy for him to see his target, which lay like a fat red eye on the matted grass of Perth Municipal Airport. But Roger's fall entranced him. It was the trip of trips, an emptying of all consciousness and reason, a dismissal of weight and matter. Roger closed his eyes. He wondered if this is how he had felt coming down the birth canal, being born now a second time.

Roger drifted. He drifted some more. When he opened his eyes, he looked for the target, but it was over there, not here. The wind caught him, threw him forwards, backwards, up and down. The target grew smaller and, as he descended, he looked between his knees, where tangled hydro wires lay waiting like a great electric snare. Below, his parents pointed, yelling into the air. The plane's pilot and the goggled instructor looked on in horror as Roger kept falling, falling, and falling until his body landed crucified on the hot trunk wires, and 44,000 volts of electricity rippled into his bones. Rescue workers eventually reached him, pulleying his body to earth. As they did, they heard a hollow *shunk* that made the hydro pole shiver. Two miles away, Bonzo's drums slurved to rest on Jennifer's turntable. The lights flickered off in the Old Persons' house, an eclipse of another kind. The young girl awoke for a moment, then went back to sleep. Lots of time left before she headed to Toronto.

On Monday, a teenager named Doug McClement pushed his long hair back on his shoulders, righted the glasses he'd worn since he was a kid, and wrote in his diary: "Back to school. Got

40% on an economics exam. Worked 6-10 p.m." A few days later, he "took Glenna MacKenzie to see Jesse Winchester at the Razor's Edge." The next day, he "bought a Sony 336 tape deck," trading in his Wharfedale W30D speaker.

When Doug wasn't being anything other than a typical sixteen-year-old kid living in Kingston, he was schlepping his bass amp into the ass-end of whatever crappy van Country Comfort used to travel from gig to gig. Despite all that was happening in his city and his country and the world, Doug's concerns were mostly musical. He was already starting to feel a little left behind, because, he remembered: "The times were changing huge in 1972. Rock and roll was growing up, maturing. After awhile, we were playing 170 nights a year, which was a lot considering that I was going to university at the time. When I'd first started playing around Ontario in the late sixties, it was very different. You'd do three forty-minute sets, and then two twenty-minute sets. You got the attention of agents and managers by going to their offices and playing for them. My band did this once, for the agent Billy O'Connor, at a place on Gerrard Street, near Maple Leaf Gardens. Seventy-one was actually the beginning of it, when the drinking age went down from twenty-one to eighteen. Bars were switching from country and folk acts to rock acts, and, on the first night of the lowered drinking age, I remember going into the Frontenac Hotel and a waiter asking me, 'So what do you want?' I remember telling him, 'Umm, I don't really know.' Our gigs changed. Before the new clubs opened up, we acted as a back-up band for strippers in places like The Village

Pump in Shannonville. At the New Byrne Hotel, which was in Arnprior, the girls would put money in the jukebox and dance to their favourite songs and, sometimes, if the song ended, they had to reach over and put in more money. We played with one stripper whose nickname was 'The Tempest' and she would come out of a coffin. We also backed up a six-foot-four black woman who used the handle 'Rikki Covette, the World's Tallest Stripper.' There was a band called Mainline, which featured Mike McKenna and Mendelson Joe, and they used to play a burlesque show called the Bump N Grind Revue at a place called the Victory. That ended in '72. It was the last vestige of that scene and that vibe, of the old Toronto Telecaster blues sound. Everything was different after 1972. I remember seeing Hall and Oates and noticing that they had road cases, whereas before, bands carried their stuff in old circus, or railway, trunks. Seventy-two was the end of the sixties DIY mentality. Bands now had sound technicians and monitors; semi-pro lighting rather than using Christmas spotlights stolen off their neighbours' front yards. The Stones tour was the first hugely grossing rock and roll tour. And we all know how that monstrosity turned out."

on monday, the beast rested. things had started badly in vancouver, when the band was denied permission to land in british columbia. officials cited errors in the flight manifest, so they called in trudeau to help, but he was fuckin' useless. the band was forced to land in washington state, run the gauntlet of customs, and when they arrived at pacific coliseum, the vagabonds were attacking the cops, two thousand non-ticket holders savaging the entrance to the arena by hurling bottles, rocks and, according to philip norman, huge lumps of iron. the city said no more of them ever, and no led zeppelin either, which meant that robert plant would never see nat bailey stadium, as if he gave a fuck in the first place. from there, the biggest tour of all time moved on, dragging countless fans and whores and dope dealers and doctors and chefs and soul vampires and robert frank and truman capote, all of them like filthy tassels on the fringe of a old weathered robe hung with rhinestones and coke spoons. big was its mantra; big was its engine. summer crowds from knoxville to fort worth to chicago watched suntanned and barefoot and stoned and horny, or so they looked flashing on tv screens across north america when we watched the news after supper: gawd don't let them go towards that, thought mom and dad, biting their nails. there were drug busts and fights and it was all dirty really dirty. the kids were camel-toed and devil-horned, juiced by radio ads with the sound of jetplane engines going *nnrrgggrrrrrr* to the throaty growl of the former bandstand announcer who would die horribly of esophagal cancer a few years later. the sign through the windshield dust said cincinnati this way as the buses shot north, trundling and nodding at high speeds. the beast was bloated, fat, but you could see its ribs and its cock if you looked closely. that summer, everyone looked closely. it was the stones. it was '72. it was the exile tour. they slouched into ohio.

———

On Monday, Al Mair was less busy than he was on most days. His star client, Gordon Lightfoot, hadn't been touring much, having removed himself from performances after his episode with Bell's palsy. But the respite was okay with Mair. Most of his life had already been consumed by rock and roll, humping records in the days when the business was only just being born. "When I first started," he said, "I would call a radio station and play them a single on the phone. If they promised to add it to their playlist, I'd mail it to them. If they received it, but didn't add it, I was expected to ask them to return it. A single manufacturing cost was ten or fifteen cents, so the long-distance call would have been more expensive than writing it off. We sold 121 copies of 'Love Me Do' when it first came out. It was a stiff until the re-release. The only place it got played was on CFRB's 'Calling All Britons.'

"I worked for a week at London Records. Their Ontario distributer, Max Zimmerman, had got into the record business when he ran a variety store on Queen Street, selling vinyl. Back then, I owned a red convertible that had a record player under the dash. The tone arm was heavy so that the record wouldn't skip when I drove, but it destroyed the vinyl. Still, the music sounded great coming out of those speakers. I'd park outside at the drive-in restaurant at Six Points Plaza in Etobicoke and play records like 'Since I Met You Baby' by Ivory Joe Hunter, 'Don't Worry Baby' by the Beach Boys, 'Let's Go, Let's Go, Let's Go' by Hank Ballard and the Midnighters, and an obscure instrumental called 'Straight Flush' by the Frantics. Local bands would play at places like the Concord Tavern. The Concord was where Ronnie Hawkins did his shows, and Saturday afternoons were all the rage. There was a dance floor in the middle, and, on one side, kids could get soda pop and chips for fifty cents, and on the other side, you could drink, although the line often blurred. You'd bring in a mickey and everyone would have a great time. Ronnie would bring up all of these great Southern rock and roll guys – guys like Ersel Hickey and Bobby Schwab (a.k.a. Bobby Starr) – and moon-walk across the stage wearing a beautiful suit. It was the beginning of what is now the Toronto rock and roll scene, where you have thousands of bands playing, everything happening seven nights a week. But back then, there was the Hawk and a few others. But that was it. It was all very new. I can't say that, by the seventies, it was old. But it had definitely changed. The business, the music, everything."

On Monday, Lightfoot himself rested, most likely in his apartment in the roundhouse building behind the Gardens, or maybe in the apartment across from it, which had only a desk and a chair, perhaps some art supplies that his friend – the painter and writer Robert Markle – had left behind. Nineteen seventy-two had been a hard year for Lightfoot. First, there was the '71 Grammys debacle, the residue of which he still felt. Organizers had asked him to play his slow, aching hit ballad, "If You Could Read My Mind," on their worldwide

awards broadcast, but there was a caveat: the show runners wanted to know if he'd consider cutting it to under two minutes, providing advertisers the time required to sell stuff to a generation that loved stuff more than any other. Canada's most famous and important songwriter — at least that's what he'd been before *Harvest, Blue,* and *Music From Big Pink,* although he'd always be the first, no matter what anyone else did — paused a moment (although it was probably even less than that) to decide that if he was going to take shit from anyone, it sure as hell wouldn't be the American Academy of the Recording Arts, or whatever ill-begotten group dictated the musical tastes of its nation. His refusal meant that he'd be dropped from the show, denying himself an international TV audience. No one knows how much anxiety this may have caused him, but according to his old manager, Al Mair, it didn't register within his organization. "To be honest, I don't really remember there being much of a fuss, at least internally. But then again, Gordon did whatever he wanted. He made the decisions and wanted to be in control of every aspect of his career."

A few months later, something else happened that may or may not have been caused by what happened before. On the first evening of a five-night run at Toronto's Massey Hall, Lightfoot felt numbness consume the left side of his face. After finishing the first set, he saw his doctor, who happened to be in the crowd. The doctor told him that he had Bell's palsy, a paralysis of the facial nerve that limits one's ability to control muscles in the face. Bell's palsy is commonly caused by trauma and emotional disorder, and while Lightfoot could rage and get wild and let everything fall loose with the best of them, he was also a bottled-up soul. "Gord wasn't the easiest person to know," remembers Mair, "which is why those nights on stage were so important to him. He lived for performing. It was his air, his food, his reason for living." Proof of this can be found in the fact that despite having to sing out of one side of his face, Lightfoot honoured his Massey Hall commitment, playing the remaining five nights. After each show, he returned to the apartment that he shared with Cathy Evelyn Smith. "Being famous isn't easy, not for anyone, even though it might look like it from the outside," said Mair. "Cathy was beautiful and smart, but she was a tramp. During that time, she was all that Gord had. And for a few years, they were virtually insepar-able. Whether this was good or bad for him depends on your perspective." In 1978, Mair told a Canadian magazine that "Gordon is one of your bigger male chauvinists and a leading exponent of the double standard. He will not do anything for nothing, for anyone." Hearing these words repeated to him years later, Mair regrets having made these remarks in public, although, he says, "it doesn't mean that they were untrue."

By the time the ball game was over (the Petes beat the Sabres, 10–2) the men had escaped: fourteen of them, in the largest prison break in Ontario history. The guard who discovered the small holes in the fence felt as if the prisoners had vanished into thin air, but the escape was more calculated than that. And it's not like no one had seen it coming. Charles Boomer, serving thirty-seven years for armed robbery, used to walk around telling anyone who would listen to him: "Fellas, I'm going on holidays."

What happened was this: during the softball game, the men had wandered into a corner blind to at least one of the roving tower floodlights. They'd clipped through the fence while the crowd cheered the folly of their fellow inmates. The men rolled past three spools of barbed wire at the bottom of the fence – to this day, no one is sure how they avoided being eviscerated – and fled into the bush a few hundred feet away. Among the escapees was Streto Dzambas. He was twenty-five years old but looked ten years older, serving a life sentence after beating a Yonge Street dishwasher, Trevor Poll, to death with a crowbar, leaving him to die on the wet kitchen floor before reaching into Poll's trousers for the fifty bucks he kept on hand in case he wanted a seat at the Chinese card game on Spadina. Running towards the prison's surrounding fields – and the neighbourhoods beyond them – Dzambas felt another convict, Ronald Fillion, moving tight at his heels. Both men were close to hyperventilating – hot lungs pounding against their throats – and it wasn't until they were a distance from the prison walls that they noticed a low fog descending, a vision that gave them comfort within their panic. Dzambas ran and Ronald ran closer, breaking with the group's plan to disperse. But the killer had already accounted for this kind of transgression, knowing that while Ronald might have been young and crazy enough to clip the wires, even though it meant risking a lifetime in prison, he was also too weak and terrified to ever suffer being alone once he was outside. Ron shouted with boyish fervour, "Streets, we did it!" breaking another rule: to be as quiet as possible while fleeing. For Dzambas, this was too much. He tightened his fists at his sides and swung, a crack shattering the stillness of the night. Ronald slunk to the earth, grabbing his face as the sound of Dzambas' footsteps thinned with every stride. Pressing the flat of his hand against his cheek, the boy stood up and tried to find his balance even though the world was bent sideways. He sensed the soft field under him; he'd forgotten what grass felt like and how it smelled in the summertime: pure and new and damp. Inspired, Ronald had a notion that he might run forever, and it's what he started to do. But something seized inside him. He vomited, then collapsed, losing five minutes before getting up and running again.

On Monday, John Singleton did something he'd been wanting to do ever since he was arrested and sent to prison three years before. There hadn't been a major escape from Collins Bay — fifteen miles west of Millhaven — for years, so he figured that the place was vulnerable, and that maybe he could surprise the guards if he tried. Cutting through the fence, he ran from the prison grounds before slowing to a walk along the CN rail line near Ernestown Station, turning east towards Kingston instead of west to Belleville. The fugitive walked and walked, or rather, he floated: barefoot across the long grass beside the dark forest stand. He walked and he walked some more before he came upon a tracking dog, who charged at his heels. Then a cadre of OPP officers appeared, shouting, guns drawn. They were part of the largest manhunt in Canadian prison history, if a manhunt in search of someone other than him.

In Monday's late edition, the *Globe and Mail* reported that "one of the big losers in the 14-man breakout was the prison's softball team, which lost its top pitcher, Richard 'Buddy' Smith, thirty-two, of Petrolia. Smith had appeared in all sixteen Circle Softball League games for the prison team before joining the others who escaped from prison. The escape came after Smith suffered his worst defeat of the season. The loss cost the Sabres sole possession of first place in the seven-team league. Murray Black, who smashed a home run and two singles off Smith, said after the game: 'I wouldn't say that he (Smith) was jittery, however, I don't think he was himself. He didn't move the ball around at all, just throwing straight strikes. I was talking to him after and I told him that I'd see him Thursday (for the next game). But Smith didn't answer. He just grinned. Now I know why.'"

LETTER IN WHICH I ASK YOU ABOUT PLAYING MASSEY HALL AND STUFF

Hey, Gord. This is the beginning of the letter. I'm not going to begin where normal biographies begin, because, I dunno, all of those books that go on to describe the legend playing with his toys and burning his hand on the stovetop and how his Grade Three teacher threw a ruler at him and the time he wet his pants coming home from school and what his dog's name was and how he saw his uncle die in a horrible chipper accident and what he did when he got his first report card; I dunno. Me, I always want the writer to get to the reasons why anyone would write a book about that person in the first place. Which, in your case, is the music, and the songs. Guitar playing. Words. Concerts. Radio. Canada. Mariposa. Drugs and love and booze. And other stuff.

So I think we should start with me imagining you being a kid like any other pre-teen kid, sitting on the quilt at the edge of your bed dressed in ill-fitting brown cords that your mom

bought for you at the Buy Right, playing a guitar that came out
of a long cardboard box, trying to find great sweeping chords
to match the fullness of the infinite sky, even though the sound
that you made was more like *sprrrngggtt!* because your hands
hurt and the tips of your fingers were sore but screw it: your
grandparents and their grandparents and their grandparents
before them had dug their mitts deep into the hard rich soil to
build a life for their sons and daughters, and because they did,
you sat there and you kept on playing: an A chord struck with
the E string accidentally opened that released a long wide note
at the bottom of the neck which made you think of a tern
swallowed by the water's horizon as your mom tapped on the
door and told you, "Phone call, son. It's Whelan," (I know your
friend's name was Whelan because it was written in that other
book about you, the one by Maynard Collins called *If You Could
Read His Mind,* which he published thirty years ago). You spoke
to Whelan, then returned to your room where you leaned
your guitar on the cowboy-wallpapered wall and slipped on
your boots and walked over to your friend's house ("Bye,
Mom"), where you played board games with him at the kitchen
table. Whelan said that he liked that new song by that skinny
guy with the goatee, Buddy Knox, but you weren't sure. No
gulls. No lakes. No silence. You were twelve, I think. Life was
moving forward, though damned if you knew where.

You liked to sing and you liked to run. I did too. Don't all
twelve-year-olds? Well, maybe not Glenn Gould, but still. You
went to junior choir practice at St. Paul's United Church in
Orillia. I imagine the old pastor dressed in dark robes taking

you aside and telling you that you sang like an angel, and just hearing him say the word – *angel* – gave you a funny feeling: a soft word coming from such a severe man, a word he'd let pass through his lips and over his teeth because your voice had somehow found a place between his rib cage and heart and maybe it was then that you understood how music worked and why it had lasted forever, despite the changing world and dinosaurs and history and war and love and God. I read somewhere that you sang high – way high – filling neighbourhood churches as the congregation swooned to the sound of your voice twirling about the moulding at the top of the church columns the way Aretha Franklin's or Little Richard's or Sam Cooke's did, although you didn't know the names of those people, not yet. Besides, their voices had been boiled in the dirty heat of the American South while yours had been born in the seizing cold, something you didn't know, either, not yet, and maybe you're realizing this for the first time here, but maybe not, because I have no idea whether you're reading this. During church service, you could see your mom and dad sitting in the pews – Mom looking proud and Dad, well, Dad just being Dad, as all dads just are – as you raised your chin with your hands hanging like scarves at your sides and you felt your diaphragm fill then empty then fill again the way your uncle worked the bellow raising fire from the hearth. At West Ward public school, they played a recording of you singing "An Irish Lullaby" over the public address system to your friends and classmates and teachers during Parents' Day; pretty much the whole town standing there listening as your soprano rang through the speaker grills at the front of those dry yellow classrooms. If your school was anything like mine – or my kids,' come to think of it – your principal was named either King or Jenkins or Arnold (they were all English back then, the principals), and what you couldn't see was how his mien softened as he spared a moment to listen to the tune you'd learned from the prized Weavers record that you played three times a day and once at bedtime on your family's four-in-one.

And then, a few years later, you were in Massey Hall. I played there, too. Just saying the name makes me shiver and I wonder if it still makes you shiver, having played it so many times over the years. It was the first time you sang in the big city, wasn't it? Shuter Street. Allan Gardens. The subway. Simpson's. Fran's. Le Coq D'Or. City Hall. You were just down the block from Maple Leaf Gardens, where Teeder Kennedy played and where that woman used to clang her bell and yell "Let's go Teeeeeder!" whenever he cupped the puck on his stick and charged up the ice. I know this meant something to you, Gord, because in 1993, they made you a celebrity captain of the Toronto Maple Leafs, and I also know that you used to go to games all the time in the seventies and eighties because Bill's mom saw you there, just hanging out, no big deal, signing autographs and talking trade. Cathy Evelyn Smith – more on her, lots more, later – also wrote that "hockey games at Maple Leaf Gardens became part of the ritual. Hoarse from cheering, we'd trudge home to the apartment through the snow." I don't know if you know it, Gord, but I love the Leafs, too. Love. I get flak for it – who doesn't? – especially when I'm on the road playing gigs or doing book tours, but I wonder whether anyone makes fun when you're around, being a legend and everything. Once, this dude came up to me after a show and was all gushing about our songs and our albums and our concerts, and then, before he left, he said, "Shame that you're a Leafs fan, though." I think he was a Habs fan, but I'm not sure. Fuckin' Habs. Do you hate them as much as I hate them, Gord? If you're a real Leafs fan – which, again, according to Bill's mom, you are – then you probably hate 'em, too. Oh yeah: even if you don't want to talk to me about music or your life, Gord, I'd be happy to sit around and bash the Habs silly. That way we could avoid talking about anything real, even though talking about hockey is realer than most things, if you know what I mean.

So there you were in Massey Hall. You smelled the hall's wood, took in the warmth of the oak balustrades, the cushioned seats. You noticed the light of the falling day refract through the stained glass windows in the upper balcony and, at once, the place felt more like home than it had any right to be: something so big, yet so small; so many people so far away, yet so close. Hours later, after everyone had arrived wearing fine Eaton's suits and dresses bought after a pause to consider the appropriate nature of such an extravagant purchase, you walked on stage, rooted yourself at the centre of the choir and you sang, your voice finding the height of the theatre's round ceiling and staying there; harmonies born one over the other and floating, hands chained, above the crowd. It was a competition and you won: first place in the Boy's Open Category for Unchanged Voices, the Kiwanis Music Festival.

After it was done, you were back in the car with your mom and dad and older sister, Beverly, and it was late evening and you thought that maybe something had changed, but maybe something hadn't. Your dad worked the steering wheel and fiddled with the radio and then he looked at you in the rear-view mirror before saying "Good work tonight, son." Or maybe he didn't tell you anything, being a man of few words. That's what they say about your dad: silent, authoritarian, as complicated as any man who walked the Earth. He used to hit you with a hairbrush. Or was it a belt? Or a strap? I've read stories where each of these are described. I also know that, one night, you took the brush or belt or strap and buried it in the backyard in an act of resolute defiance that would shadow pretty much everything you did in your life, good and bad. Maynard Collins (and Jason Schneider, too, in a book called *Whispering Pines*, which is about you and Neil Young and Ian and Sylvia and others) said that your dad used to work in a bank, and that it was a good job, but that when the bosses found out that he was engaged to your mom, they fired him. Apparently, they wanted single men in their employ, which seems stupid, but those were different times. He got a job at Wagg's Laundry – a job he didn't like much, but really, who likes their job? – and that's where he stayed until he retired. I don't know if he was proud of you, but, like I said, parents have a funny way of expressing themselves. Still, during that car ride home, maybe it was what he didn't say that mattered most. Maybe by saying nothing, he was saying this: all kids are angels, son, and your wings are steady, sure, but just because you can sing, that doesn't mean you can fly. Not yet. Still, the old man stopped at the Severn Hotel. You ordered frog's legs, and toasted winning with ginger ale. The bubbles popped hot against your throat. Sometimes parents say the weirdest things. Sometimes what's weirdest is what they don't say at all.

TUESDAY, JULY 11TH

On Tuesday, Anand Chopra, thirty-two, was, according to the *Toronto Star,* "driving east on Bloor Street when he saw a man standing naked on the wall of the Bloor Viaduct" above the city's Don Valley, a popular spot for jumpers before a protective fence was built in 2003. Mr. Chopra said, "People were passing as though nothing was wrong, even though the man had thrown his clothes into the Don River. I decided right then that it didn't matter if someone hit my car, so I stopped, ran across to him, and grabbed him by the legs just as he started to jump. Then, another man came to help. I was shocked that nobody else had come to talk to him." Chopra remembers that "the man was in tears. He was so happy that we saved him. He told me that he was depressed. He said that he just wanted someone to talk to."

On Tuesday, Team Canada (and ex-Bruins') coach Harry Sinden answered the goddamned phone in his goddamned hotel suite in goddamned Toronto in the middle of goddamned July, the heart of the summer, which was supposed to be about burgers and fishing and broads and beers and driving down a gravel road going nowhere, but instead, it was about this god-damned hockey series against the goddamned Russians. The *Star*'s Proudfoot was calling. Harry told him, as he'd told him countless goddamned times before, "This is my team. And Bobby Hull will be on it."

On Tuesday, tall, ponytailed Brent Titcomb drove around France. Brent had arrived there from England via Canada, the totem of a scarab beetle stuffed in the pocket of his jeans. He was thirty-two years old and had already spent years playing in Yorkville, which he described as "a place where you parked your ideas, exchanged thoughts and music and philosophies with other people your own age." If, by 1972, the idyll had started to rust for others, it hadn't for Brent, who talked about how there were safe houses on every block; psychedelic drop-ins where, he said, "you'd sit around and get into heavy discus-sions about life and art, something that I just don't see in today's generation of kids. It was a euphoric time, and music was changing. Someone would go down to Sam the Record Man and pick up an album and we'd sit around, getting high and listening to it over and over. *Sergeant Pepper's Lonely Hearts Club Band* was like that. You'd hear words you'd never heard before in a song, and instruments that you never knew existed. *Music from Big Pink* was the same. I remember hearing about it and thinking, 'They recorded their album *in a house?*' It just wasn't done before. There was Joni, too, and her crazy tunings, and the voices in CSNY: such strange harmonic structures. Before Dylan and The Band and the Byrds, we'd never heard folk music that had bass and drums before. Those musicians — as well as Ian and Sylvia and Lightfoot — made us realize that we didn't only have to cover songs by other artists; we could write our own. It might seem standard now, but things that are regarded as a given today were actually pretty revolutionary back then. The world was changing before our eyes and I was lucky to be part of it."

Brent awoke on the morning of his trip in a home he shared with producer/guitarist Brian Ahern, who would later meet and wed singer Emmylou Harris. Heading to the airport, he realized that he only had two contacts in the U.K., one of whom was a woman named Carol. "I could have phoned either of the numbers," he said. "But I called Carol. When she answered, she told me that if I could get to her place in forty-five minutes, I could go with her to meet the Chief Druid, a fellow named Thomas Maughm. It seemed like as good a plan as any.

"Thomas Maughm had a long white beard and eyes that, when he flashed them, pierced you like electric shocks. He was dressed normally, but he looked like something out of *Lord of the Rings*. He had a very deep, ethereal quality and there were people around him who were entranced by his presence. Some were so overwhelmed that they couldn't even look at him. Me, because I'd just landed, and because I didn't really understand or know about his reputation, I treated him normally. We were just hanging out. We walked through the garden and talked and then he asked us to stay for dinner. I couldn't have known it at the time, but meeting him was the beginning of a remarkable few weeks. Looking back, it was as if meeting him was a preparation for all that was about to happen."

After a few days, Brent met a group of people who said they were going to a place called Worthy Farm, in Glastonbury, to attend a new rock festival. Brent joined their caravan, dropping by the home of scholar John Bennett's, who'd already left for the festival site. John was a disciple of George Ivanovich Gurdjieff, who was a mystic and a spiritual teacher and whose "Fourth Way" dogma – borrowed from the Sufi's concept of self-awareness – had attracted a legion of followers. Gurdjieff – and Bennett – believed that the world had become stunted as a result of people having lost their ability to perceive reality, their lack of consciousness supplanted by a kind of hypnosis, or, in Gurdjieff's words, "a waking sleep." Brent and his new friends discussed these concepts as they rolled through the English countryside. "Between hearing about John, and my encounters with the Chief Druid, I found myself immersed in a world of spiritually and mysticism. And when we got to Glastonbury, I felt more energized and alive – and awake – than I'd been in my entire life."

At Worthy Farm, Titcomb put this energy to work. "We arrived early to the festival. The weather was torrential, and it wasn't long before I realized that these English kids had no idea how to build shelters for us, especially considering what had become of the ground: a great, muddy soup that made it hard to move around. So I went into town to the local hardware store and got some twine, plastic and, with saplings, built something that looked like an igloo – a snow lodge, at least – using rocks to hold down the plastic covering. It was basically what I'd learned to do as a kid growing up in the forests around West Vancouver, and while everyone was really impressed and grateful, it's something I would have done anyway. The entrance was like an igloo's, except that it curved around so that the wind wouldn't get in. I lit candles to heat the place, and I was really comfortable. Outside, the wind was howling at great speeds and the rain made it seem as if the Earth was about to end.

"The festival organizers wanted to build the stage using the proportions of the Great Pyramid. They placed the stage at the epicentre of two very heavy lay lines – also known as planetary meridians of energy – that crossed in the middle of the farm. There was a great concern over what kind of energies would be invoked, so they moved it slightly off-centre. The terrible weather persisted, so someone had the idea to drive a stake into the exact centre of where the lines crossed. Almost immediately, the skies cleared. It was freaky. Then, after they'd built everything, they needed someone to test the sound system and they came round to my shelter and asked if I'd help. I said sure. Not many people know it, but I was the first person to ever play live music at what is now regarded as the most famous musical festival in Europe.

"One of the reasons for going to Europe was to rescue my wife. She'd gotten into trouble and had fallen ill. She'd been working at Bill Wyman's place in Nice, where the Stones were recording *Exile on Main Street*. After I got her, I knew that I had to get back quickly because of my date at Mariposa, so I dowsed to find out when I should return. You see, a dowser asks themselves questions with only yes or no answers, and I was told to fly home on the day of my gig. It seemed crazy – flying from England on the morning of a show in another country – but that's what I did. When I landed in Toronto, I went straight to my set, arriving twenty minutes late. On stage, I told the crowd, 'You might not believe me, but I woke up this morning in Kent, England, and now, folks, here I am.' Of course, everybody probably thought it was just a story, just a line, but it was true. When I finished my set, I walked down the steps from the stage. Standing at the bottom was Joni Mitchell, looking up at me."

If life had been upended at home, things were changing in other places, too, like Iceland, where, on Tuesday, people expected something to happen that hadn't happened in thirty years: an American sitting across from a Russian, fingers tented, heads bowed, trying to read the intimacy of each other's thoughts in an intellectual pas de deux that would become the focus of their respective nations' attention.

That morning, Bobby Fischer, the American challenger, was scheduled to start play against Boris Spassky, the Russian champion, in a twenty-game chess summit. The opening games would be broadcast around the world, and while both men had arrived in Reykjavik, Fischer refused to come to the table. He kept demanding more money. His behaviour fomented outrage in the Soviets, who were loathe to endure delay after delay after delay. They pressed the federation to penalize Fischer with a one-game loss. They argued that Spassky, the champion, was deeply troubled and his focus upset by Fischer's obvious gamesmanship. The Russians eventually settled on a personal letter of apology from Fischer – he wrote and delivered two of them – and one imagines the American giggling behind his hand as he watched the pot swell to a quarter of a million dollars, the difference provided by James Slater, a British financier and chess aficionado.

Just after dawn in an exhibition hall in the Icelandic capital, two thousand fans (some of whom had lined up at five in the morning to view the match) watched as Spassky – sporting a neutral haircut and dressed in a sombre suit and vest – moved into his chair to await the arrival of his opponent, who, despite being placated by the increased prize money, was still nowhere to be found. The Russian moved his white pawn anyway, then lowered his head and held it there until Fischer finally made his entrance. The American came into the hall seven minutes late, sat hunched over the board, snorted to himself, then made his first move. Downstairs, in the cafeteria, hundreds of fans watched on closed-circuit television, eating breakfast and drinking beer. They watched closer still as the American, after a few more moves, stood up, sought the attention of match officials, and waved a finger at them: the blue, white, and red emblem of the International Chess Federation had become a major distraction, to say nothing of the orange juice, which was lukewarm, and could the organizers please find him some ice cubes? They did (of course they did) and the game continued. Actually, it exploded, with Fischer taking Spassky's poisoned pawn, leaving his own bishop exposed and risking a move that would almost certainly lead to clear victory for either player, as opposed to the draw to which both men appeared headed. People debated Fischer's tactics. Was it cunning? Crazy? Manipulative? Wrong-headed? Was Fischer sacrificing the game to build false confidence in his opponent, or was he simply overmatched? The crowd in the cafeteria drained their beers, ordered more. Those sitting in the hall tried to quiet their pounding hearts. Spassky moved and waited for Fischer to respond, but instead, the American rose from his chair and demanded that the television crew working from the side of the stage be asked to leave immediately. Why move them now? asked the organizers. Why not now? said Fischer. Really? C'mon. Jesus. Yes, now. Really. The organizers refused. Fischer walked out, losing thirty-five minutes from his time limit. Eventually, his request was granted (of course it was). Returning to the room, he was forced to make sixteen moves in twenty-five minutes, all of them in vain. The game was suspended and played out the next morning, but Fischer had already thrown it into the hands of the reigning world champion. And so: Russia: 1; Capitalists: 0.

———

On Tuesday, two bachelor farmers, Ray and Bill Newbury, sat in the drawing room of the farmhouse they shared with their seventy-one-year-old mother. Like everyone in the greater Kingston area, the mass escape from the nearby prison made the Newburys see and hear things differently: the long grass rustling a little too hard; a bird's cry jangling with alarm; and the soft sweep of the wind growing rough and fingernailed as it crept through old doors and window frames. Homes had been locked down, roads closed, and the area's perimeter secured by a police force trying not to panic. In the July 12th edition of the *Toronto Star,* a photograph on the front page showed fourteen-year-old Paul Battersby with his dog, Pal, cradling a double-barrelled shotgun while sitting on his front porch, ready to defend his sister, twelve-year-old Andrea, should the convicts come to take them hostage (the Battersby parents were on vacation at the time). On nearby Wolfe Island – a twenty-minute ferry ride from the Kingston mainland – a group of men lined the edge of the dock with rifles, although no one could be certain that the fugitives hadn't already crossed.

Dairy farming was the Newbury brothers' vocation. It was their life, and all they ever knew. The brothers kept forty Holsteins, and, prison escape or otherwise, the cows had to be milked. They knew their animals, knew them well, and so those strange sounds – a knocking that happened once, then not again; a depth of lowing that lasted longer than it would have under normal circumstances – all of these things made the Newbury brothers turn to each other before they bundled their mother into their car, drove her to a neighbour's house, and returned home to step softly, quietly, through the low grass towards the barn behind the farmhouse, their two shot-guns pointing dead-eyed at the wooden doors.

On Tuesday, Colin Linden came home from school and went straight into the basement. He grabbed his guitar and started practising in the suburban home that he shared with his mom and brother. Colin practised all of the time, every day. The previous morning, Colin's mom had suggested that he head down to Mariposa on the weekend to play the Open Mic stage, even though he'd never performed in front of anyone before. Colin said he'd think about it. The extra bedroom in their North York home had been turned into the music room, empty of furniture save for a small oak desk – good for lyric writing – a record player, and Colin's first guitar. In the corner, there was also a couch that rolled out into a bed, and that suited Colin, too: a place where, after hours of playing – his young fingers having contorted into strange new shapes on the un-forgiving fretboard – he could stretch out and imagine that, instead of being twelve years old and seasoned in nothing but sugared cereal, television, and comic books, he was a hard-ened gig-slave rumbling down the interstate on the back bench of a bus or luxury sedan. In his dreams, he was a ragged blues-man, even though he hadn't even touched his first tit.

———

For Bobby Hull, the star hockey player, tits were everywhere. He couldn't help himself: they just were. In the seventies, tits bounced across the mainstream: in *Klute* with Jane Fonda; in the films of Russ Meyer; on Paula Prentiss in *The Parallax View,* which I saw with my parents on holidays in the U.S.A.; in R. Crumb's comic books; in the softcore Baby Blue Movies that Citytv showed on Friday nights; in *Playboy, Penthouse, Cheri, Oui,* and *Swank* magazines, which the neighbourhood smoke-and-gift racked on the top shelf; on Blind Faith, Roxy Music, and Jimi Hendrix album covers; and on the occasional female streaker, who, whenever she passed across the news, disappeared into the darkness of my parents' palms clapped across my eyes.

They called Bobby the Golden Jet. He'd won a Stanley Cup in 1961, and, over the years, had become hockey's first playboy. When he signed his enormous million-dollar novelty cheque with the new rogue hockey league – the WHA – his Winnipeg team decided to name themselves after him. Women were everywhere. Chicks wanted him and guys wanted to know him. He paid a small fortune to have golden hair plugs sutured into his head before outfitting himself in suede and velour and signing endorsement deals with clothiers, equip-ment manufacturers, pizza joints, and jewellers way before players did that sort of thing. He always had a big chuckling smile for the autograph boys, a strong handshake for the dads, and a low, sharkish leer for the ponies and the moms. Bobby Hull was seventies hockey personified. His slapshot was the broadest gesture of widescreen power in a game looking for its telegenic money shot. He wanted everything and he wanted it now, but he was just doing as any seventies über-dude would have done. His new league and his new team would start in the fall, but first he'd play against the Russians. He'd show those Commie bastards his banana blade. He'd feed them his shot and make them wish they'd never laid eyes on such a great and glorious Canadian specimen: rich, straight-toothed, farm-raised, and equine-strong. He'd drive Yuri and Sergei and Igor all the way back to the Turkmeni mountains. Their Svetlanas, he'd keep behind.

On Tuesday, another famous Canadian playboy – Pierre Elliott Trudeau, who, at fifty-two, was still cool and sideburned, yet, on this day, looking slightly sallow-cheeked and weary-eyed – spared himself a moment to think of nothing. The polls, the newspapers, and the pundits all suggested that the end of Trudeaumania was near, and if that wasn't bad enough, he'd been consigned to visit Prescott, not far from the site of the Millhaven escape, to unofficially kick off an election campaign that would result in his governing party losing its grip on power, forfeiting a majority government, and ensuring that the NDP would influence any decision made by cabinet.

If the sixties had been about unconditional free-spiritedness – about the folly of doing something just because it was impulsive and hip and, allegedly, "free" – the relative ennui of the 1970s forced people to walk behind the curtain, bored and in search of a new buzz. The headline in Tuesday's

Globe and Mail read, "PM RUNS INTO THUNDER, BROKEN HARNESS, PUZZLING QUESTIONS," its words possessing considerably less fervour than back in the day when all Trudeau had to do was flash a tuft of chest hair or sniff a rose to get the nation's panties wet. In 1968, Trudeau visited Centre Island for a Metro Liberal Party picnic, where, according to Sally Gibson, he "shook hands with the faithful, danced with Miss Toronto, planted kisses on willing cheeks, and was adorned with two leis." A few years later, in 1971, he was jeered by protestors along the same shoreline for refusing to acknowledge the rights of island residents.

The Prime Minister's weekend had started in Brockville – no story would ever be worth telling with that kind of beginning, P.E.T. might have thought to himself – and if he'd performed his duties with a kind of natural aplomb (opening a military pageant, presenting the legion with a flag that had flown on the Peace Tower) there was no hiding the fact that, where he'd once executed these acts with dazzle and snap, they were now rendered by a tired leader who carried with him the wearisome burden – and knowledge – that such perfunctory tasks were now as great a part of his life as talking poetry with André Previn or architecture with Gore Vidal. Trudeau, thought Trudeau, shouldn't have been required to perform the kind of glad-handing stunts favoured by lesser politicians, even though, of course, he knew they were necessary. Still, because of the precariousness by which his party held sway – popular support for the Liberals had fallen off and the country had grown cynical of Trudeau's Machiavellian leadership and air of political divinity – in the end it might not have mattered what kinds of stunts or ceremonies he was forced to endure. If he were at all aware of his political mortality – which he must have been, considering that he would have been fed reports measuring what everyone else knew – it couldn't have been fun for Canada's leader to stand in shit-deep fields tickling babies, judging prized hogs, or doing whatever else the podunks of Brockville demanded.

Since 1968, Pierre Trudeau and Gordon Lightfoot had been the golden era's gleaming hood ornaments. Both had informed their country with a sense of identity at more or less the same time. If Trudeaumania had given way to novelty songs about sideburns and "fuddle duddle," the music that played on kitchen and cabin radios during his ascent was largely Lightfoot's. While the PM had remoulded Canada's idea of a leader, Lightfoot was his country's first natural-born star, re-shaping its sound by doing what few artists had done before: naming Canadian places and events in songs that were as melodic and interesting as anything on the charts. And if one aspect of Trudeau's legacy was the establishment of an intellectual and cultural distance between Canada and the U.S.A., Lightfoot was the first musician to win popular approval at home before getting famous in the States. Similarly, if nature, emptiness, the winter, and the endlessness of the land had once been Canadian characteristics best voiced in hushed whispers, Trudeau used them as the basis for his election platform ("The Land Is Strong") while Lightfoot's songs about railroads and snow became standard lyrical fare among folksingers. In the late sixties and early seventies, these two men – along with Bobby Orr – would define the way Canadians saw themselves then, and, in some ways, evermore.

But if Trudeau had ignited Canada like a match to a firecracker's fuse, what remained after the glow of EXPO and winning the Olympics for Montreal was a country largely pawing its way through a cloud of stale smoke. The uncertainty of Trudeau's governance represented the end of Canada's golden age, and, in 1972, there was jealousy and resentment towards a leader who'd had too much, too soon, too often. If, for instance, John Lennon and Yoko Ono's visit to 24 Sussex Drive had, for a moment, announced to young voters that a new kind of liberation was consuming Ottawa, in the end what it amounted to was nothing more than a rock star who'd shown up, had tea or coffee, then left. While both Trudeau and the cultural corporals who'd helped establish the Maple Law supported, encouraged, and were excited by the concept of change, they were also helpless to prevent whatever those changes yielded. Canada's future had been set in motion, but the thought of the wheel turning to crush those who'd pushed it forward was not unfathomable. Lightfoot, Trudeau, and Orr all suffered through their most difficult years in 1972.

During the week of July 10–16, Trudeau found himself slogging through the dreary fields of Prince Edward County under grey skies and pouring rain, while Lightfoot remained sequestered in his apartment to deal with his Bell's palsy. For his part, Bobby Orr had just endured another in a gruesome series of knee operations while waiting to see if he would be cleared to play in the Series of the Century. The promise of the late sixties was over, if for no other reason than the initial impact of these men had already been made. All they could do was manage expectations and hope to do as little damage as possible to their reputations.

Still, as the PM prepared to fire a 212-year-old cannon in yet another ceremonial gesture designed to win unwinnable votes, the old titfucker proved that he still had some life in him. CP reported that "at the opening of Saturday's military pageant in Prescott, the master of ceremonies asked reporters and photographers to stand to the side and thirty feet away for safety reasons when Trudeau fired the cannon. Then, after a long pause, the following announcement was made: 'The Prime Minister asks that the press take their positions in front of the cannon.'"

If much of Canada was feeling disaffected with the arrogance – or ease, or confidence – with which their leader went about his business, the same could not have been said for twenty-one-year-old Jean Francis, who, on Tuesday, passed out exhausted in her parents' house in Kapuskasing. She'd spent the day at the youth hostel, which she'd been running for two summers along with a few friends. It was the only youth hostel in the greater northern area, but not the only one in Canada. Back in the late sixties, this sort of operation helped assist an enormous number of kids criss-crossing the country; hippie kids and road kids, falling out of the nest and thumbing from city to city in search of no one but each other.

Francis had received funding from Trudeau's government to run her hostel, assisting people travelling or hitchhiking or needing a place to stay. They ran it at Clear Lake, with lots of sleeping tents and a cooking tent. "It was a twenty-four-hour operation and we'd give out food as a hospitality," said Francis. "That was part of the funding, too; providing enough money to buy food to feed whoever stopped there. I came up with the idea after going to see Pierre Elliott Trudeau give a speech at the Kapuskasing airport. I was in high school at the time and everybody was yelling and screaming for him. In his speech, he said, 'You should all be travelling; you should see the world. We need to see what other people are doing and how they're living to give us insight about who we are and what we do.' He told us that travelling the world would be a better education for us than going to school. To this day, my mother blames Trudeau for me quitting university."

Francis was happy living up north, but she felt that she needed to explore other parts of the province. "That summer of '72, someone told us about the Mariposa Folk Festival and we decided to go," she said. "We drove down in the middle of the night in a 1968 Camaro. It took us eight hours. Back then, people were doing lots of MDA, and I think I bought my hit from a vendor in the crafts area. It was very clandestine, but everyone knew how and where to get it."

Like Jean Francis, Gordon Klager — twenty years old and living in Ottawa — worked at a youth hostel, in Carleton, where, he said, "there were lots of us on the payroll, and the whole thing was subsidized. We had four hundred people staying there every night. It cost fifty cents for dinner and breakfast and a place to sleep. The government also paid for buses that went out to the highway at night and picked up hitchhikers who couldn't get a ride. They brought them to us overnight, and came and picked them up the next morning, taking them back to the highway. In the late sixties and early seventies, everybody – well, every young person I knew – had a cool job created by the Trudeau government. I was within one application of getting a job driving an old hippie bus across Canada with a nurse to help people hitchhiking coast-to-coast."

Klager also remembered something called the Le Dain Commission, an endeavour bankrolled by the Liberals to examine whether or not pot was dangerous. He said that "the government had started an experimental farm near Carleton where they grew dope, and, one night, a few guys came into the hostel with bags full of pot. They'd crossed the river and harvested the stuff and no one had found out or even cared. These other friends of mine had it better than anyone. Their summer job was to go out to Rockcliffe airport at night, get stoned, and drive a bunch of cars around on the runways to measure the affects of marijuana on driving. This was the summer of 1971. A big part of Trudeau's message was 'Anything is possible.' We bought into it big time."

Trudeau was nothing if not accessible in a time when visibility and public outreach was still a large part of a politician's

m.o. In 1972, it was the PM's habit to work the press by
meeting it head on, and to win support of voters not by per-
suasive TV ads or robo-calls, but in the fields and parks and
thoroughfares where his constituents lived and played. He
went where few politicians had gone before: to the festivals,
discotheques, and soirées of the young and beautiful, often
appearing as the centrepiece of these events. Even though he
sometimes gave the impression of floating above everyone else,
he also threaded easily into the voters' worlds.

Klager remembered going to see Crowbar play in 1971
in Stewart Park in Perth. "All of the politicians were around
– guys in suits in their sixties and seventies standing next to
their wives – and there was their leader in the middle – Pierre
– wearing a cool buckskin jacket with his wife, Maggie, looking
beautiful in a long gyspy dress. Maggie and Pierre were hanging
out near the river listening to the band when a couple of
freaks in a canoe rowed past them holding a big sign that said
LEGALIZE MARIJUANA. Sometimes, people don't believe these
stories, but they're true. I was there. I saw it happen."

It would be wrong to cast Trudeau as a music junkie, but
there's no ignoring that his leadership had a direct effect on
music in Canada. For the first time, musicians were treated
the way poets and playwrights had been. They were recognized for their creativity and importance in a country once
dominated by more traditional "artists." Having Canada's
head of state attend rock shows was a huge boost for the
players and their industry, and it says something that Trudeau's
default tastes leaned to a band as outrageous as Crowbar, who

were as known for their unpretentious and cartoonish live shows as for songs like "Tits Up On the Pavement" and "Glass Full of Liquid Pain."

Once, Roly Greenway of Crowbar was on stage at the Royal York Hotel with the prime minister – "I think we were getting a gold record for 'Oh, What a Feeling!'" – and he remembered telling a story to the crowd about the time the band played the PM's rally at Maple Leaf Gardens. Afterwards, Trudeau turned to him and said, "I don't know how you remembered that. You guys are always so fucking stoned." This frankness was part of Trudeau's appeal, said Roly. "He had a mouth on him. But he spoke like you and me. He was one of the guys," he added. "He got into our music because of Margaret, who used to come to see us play in Vancouver. We didn't gig there a lot, but when we did, she'd be front and centre. She'd come in with a bunch of big burly guys, and she'd tell them, 'Lay off the band; they're okay.' We got to know each other pretty well. After we became popular, she brought Trudeau out, and we got to know him, too. Once, we were playing in Perth on a raft in the middle of the river. After our set, Sonny (Bernardi) and Kelly (Jay) went over to where Pierre and Maggie were standing. We'd been given a letter to pass on to him by the mayor of Hamilton, but, earlier in the day, we'd steamed it open, rolled two joints, and put them inside. He used to pass everything on to his staff, but when they gave him the envelope, they said, 'You might wanna keep what's inside for yourself.' He opened it up, took out the letter, and gave it to his staff. The envelope, he put in his pocket.

Afterwards, we tried fitting a crowbar over his head – a kind of rock and roll coronation, I guess – but it wouldn't go. So Maggie came over and she slid it on. She knew how to do it, just so. Later on, the press wanted to know which of us had hooked up with Maggie, and when they asked, we all pointed at each other. She was my friend. She was just a nice, happy-go-lucky girl. It's too bad that it didn't work out. I liked both of them a lot. It's not often that you can describe the leader of your country in one word, but with Maggie and Trudeau, it would be *fun*."

As Trudeau slogged home from Prescott, police and soldiers traveled through the bush around Prince Edward County. Balled up and fetal, twenty-two-year-old escaped convict Gaston Lambert had buried himself in a mound of hay in the Newbury brothers' barn, waiting for the deep night to come before moving on to god knows where. The foul stench of prison – ass and smoke and musk – was replaced by the stench of the animals – shit and sour milk and blood – and while he'd been able to at least manage his time inside by carrying a shiv in his pant leg or forming an alliance with the Newfies or trading Export A Green Deaths for other privileges, hiding in that barn reminded him how little control he had of the outside world, to say nothing of the natural world, which went its own fucking way. One cow had bellowed hard when she'd seen him come into the barn, but the beasts had calmed themselves. The hay was dry and the ground was hard. Lambert wanted to sleep, but his adrenalin bubbled. He thought he heard something outside. A pair of boots, moving slowly. Still, it could have been the madness starting. Fugitive paranoia. He'd heard that could happen.

On Tuesday, David McTaggart stared into the beautiful nothing and tried to measure his own madness. It was just after dawn in the South Pacific as his boat, the *Vega* – a forty-one-foot ketch – sliced across the sea. If his new home in New Zealand had made him fight to remember his past – years winning rich development contracts, national badminton championships, and a young life exploring the forests of British Columbia – being at the world's edge seemed to render all that had happened before irrelevant. The waters were calm and the sun grew tangerine fat on the horizon. McTaggart thought about turning on the radio and sending a message to the world, but he reconsidered. Silence. He would enjoy it while he could.

Lambert heard the footsteps coming. They were heavy, trampling the grass outside the barn. Because he was weak and hungry and filthy and afraid, they sounded monstrous to him, like something out of a terrifying children's book: attached to a creature sharp-toothed and dark-furred, great-pawed and drooling. Lambert panicked. He scuttled out the back door and fell to his stomach, where he shimmied like an amphibian across the dry grass. He swished and swished and swished until he reached a shallow gully about one hundred feet from the barn. He turned on his back and held his breath, listening. For awhile, there was only silence, but even that wasn't comforting. Then, the Newbury brothers appeared, rising terrible against the sky's panoply of stars. One of the brothers was carrying a large stick, while the other told Lambert to stand up. There was a time in Lambert's life when he'd been a strong, estimable man: left defence; iron spine; hands like cinder blocks. Once, he'd cleared an entire stand of black spruce, he and his uncle, swinging axes and sawing cordwood, then collapsing in their sleeping bags after nightfall before rising six hours later to do it again. But Lambert had to leave the country, and had grown soft. In the city, he met this guy and that guy and this guy and that guy and it seemed like the greatest opportunities were always the ones with the most risk. "Stand up. Start walking." Lambert lay there and pissed himself. "Stand up!" Lambert stood up. His feet were heavy and his crotch wet. "Stop. Against that tree. Turn around." He turned around. "I'm wet," he told them. "Stick him, Ray," said one of the men. Ray stuck him. He held the long, sharp, crooked branch against the small of Lambert's back. "I'm fucking wet." He drove the stick into Lambert until it hurt. "There, I can hear 'em," said one of the men. "About time," said the other. Twenty-five cops. Lambert stood against the tree soaked in piss. They would know what happened as soon they saw him.

———

dope there's dope go get 'em cries the voice inside the head of the ohio cop who finds himself all of a sudden surrounded by kids who have grown fangs and claws as their stoned summertime engine-work muscle rises to pull off his visor and then another cop's visor and before you know it it's vancouver all over again and here we are the stones on their exile tour trundling and trundling and trundling on. cops are falling. cops are twisted below. cops are stumbling backwards and kids are thrashing around but after awhile they don't know what to do and besides, shit man, stevie wonder is playing: brap brap brap brap on that strange keyboard thing. even though he can't see the violence rippling through the bowl he can still feel the legs of his keyboard wheeze as the stage rocks just so with surging bodies trying to either get out of the fray or into it. chip monck jumps on stage and grabs the mic and tells everybody to stop and somehow everybody stops, even stevie, although he'll start as soon as more cops have found their way to the fallen cops where they headlock the bad kids into the paddy wagon who shout pigs pigs the world is ruled by pigs. stevie will play something from his new album, talking book. he is opening for the stones in '72. in ohio, then on to canada. weird fucking gig.

LETTER IN WHICH I ASK YOU ABOUT
TRACK AND FIELD AND ROCK AND ROLL

Gord, I found this. I don't know if it means anything.

WIKIPEDIA ENTRY (EDITED)
JOHN WILFRED LOARING
John Wilfred Loaring was one of the first Canadian track stars, winning silver in the 400 metres at the Olympic Games in 1936. Loaring, who as a child in Winnipeg was stricken with but survived rheumatic fever, ran the relay, too. In the semi-final relay heat, he received the baton ahead of his fellow anchor, Rudolph Harbig, who a few years later would set world records in the 400 and 800. During the heat, Loaring slowed down so that Harbig could pass him and win in front of his countrymen. Canada would advance to the final regardless, and, in an purer age of sporting chivalry, it seemed like the jake thing to do. In the final, Canada's third runner was fouled by an American, and when he received the baton,

Loaring had already spotted Harbig a ten-metre lead. But, running down the stretch, he was able to catch him. The two runners finished together, but a review showed that the German had hit the tape first, giving the home side bronze while the Canadians finished out of the money. Officials quickly huddled to discuss the Americans' infraction, then asked Canadian team organizers if they wanted to file a protest. Worried that a protest would be perceived as ungentlemanly and sour, they told them they would not. A few weeks later, the popular German weekly, Fussball, *selected Loaring as "the toughest competitor of 1936." Noted Olympic authors Ross and Norris McWhirter commented that: "Loaring's competitive record at the 1936 Olympics . . . represent(s) the most severe test to which any Olympic athlete has ever been subjected."*

Twenty-four months later, in his last year of university, Loaring wrote his final exams early so that he could be in the first group of Royal Canadian Naval Volunteer Radar Officers on loan to the British during World War II, leaving Canada in April of 1940. In September of 1940, his destroyer was dispatched to pick up civilian survivors of a torpedoed liner. After explaining his life-saving skills to the ship's doctor, he was assigned five tiny, lifeless bodies. Three were revived under Loaring's direction, and he was commended by the Ontario Branch of The Royal Life Saving Society. He served as radar officer on H.M.C.S. Fiji, which ran out of ammunition during the Battle for Crete, and was sunk by a German bomber on May 22, 1941. Five hundred and twenty-three of the 764 naval personnel survived, clinging to wreckage until they were picked up a few hours later. Loaring was put ashore in Africa to recover from oil poisoning. He returned to Canada and settled in Windsor, Ontario, where he started a family, raising a son, John Jr., who would win the Royal Arcanum Award as Windsor's best all-round athlete.

Here's another thing. This one, I made up:

ORILLIA TIMES, MAY 24TH, 1952
BY DONALD RIVARD
Yesterday, the regional county track and field championships were contested at Simcoe Field, drawing together over 100 of the region's finest high school athletes. Multiple winners included Seth Martindale, 13, from Chincoussy High (gold medals in hurdles, 1,000 metres and pole vault) as well as Jane Rudner, 11, from Atherly Vocational (gold and silver in high jump and 50-metre dash), and Orillia's Gordon Lightfoot, 14, who captured gold in the shot put as well as a bronze medal in the 50-metre dash.

Gord, you liked to sing, but you also liked sports (did I tell you how cool that makes you seem?). Let me ask you: was it the way the field smelled at 8 a.m.? The perfume of wet earth pushed out by the clover, and how your runners felt bouncing across the new spring grass as you left the scent of your parents' kitchen in the morning, the coffee boiled and eggs frying in the pan, Mom still in her nightdress, Father fixed for Wagg's, which is where he would go to work every morning for thirty years, becoming manager, middle class, and prosperous, all things considered. The hair on your legs probably spiked at the touch of the air, which still carried a tingle of the ice locked in up the bay, the weight of the summer still months away. From what I know, you arrived first – you were always first – and the field was yours as you stretched the way you were shown in the gatefold of the physical education brochure that sat alongside the register at a place maybe called Galbraith's Cycle and Sports, the proprietor, his mane of blond hair swept across his sourdough head, wearing a white athletic shirt and dark sweat-pants with red maple leaf piping running down the leg. The volleyballs had their own smell. The boxing gloves, too. Maybe you remember Mr. Galbraith pulling out a set of new Cougars, striped brown and white, and how his hands dimpled at the knuckles fanned out like sand dollars as he grabbed you by the ankle, guiding one foot, then the other, into the shoe's bonnet, your dad standing above the Cycle and Sports fitting chair as if marshalling a math test.

Running across the field for the first time in your new shoes gave your feet life, and you felt like you were running faster than ever. At first, you were alone, then everyone else showed up: Scoot, Rocky, Mouse, Whelan, The Mole, Branch, Skerf, Jones (I made some of those names up; some of them I got from Collins' book). Whelan might have said, "They don't give out ribbons for showing up first, you know," and you tried smiling at your pal, but you could not, and because he was your friend, he understood. Later, your fists might have tightened as you walked to the starting line thinking about John Loaring – the closest anyone in the Dominion had come to being a track star – how he'd raced to catch the German running for Hitler, lost him at the finish line, then bowed his head before telling his coaches, "Let the foul ride; let it be pure victory or nothing." Maybe you thought that track and field and war were not that different, and that when he'd saved those dying men and women and, later on, thrashed about the ocean swallowing waves of oil, perhaps track and field and sports had prepared him for that; the taste of sweat and the essence of self that rises in your throat before the inevitable moment when you find yourself in the presence of death, which you must outrun, too. Waiting along the chalk line of that red-gravel track with your elbows pointing out, perhaps you thought that track and field and war (and music) were different things, but maybe you thought they were the same. I don't know.

The gun cracked.

You ran.

So: high school. Everyone has to suffer through it. I don't know what it was like for you as a musician – I can guess, and I'll tell you what I think I know in a moment – but, for me, it was like being lost in space. Outer space. I hung out with three other friends, and we were into New Wave. Does that term mean anything to you, Gord? Carol Pope. The Spoons. Synthesizers. The Police. Anyhow, my three friends and I were into New Wave while everyone else was into any kind of music that wasn't New Wave. They were into disco and hard rock – which I liked, too – but hard rock was too hard to play, at least on guitar. New Wave guitar, you see, was ideal for me. There are no really heroic or famous New Wave guitarists. It's the bassists who played the riffs. New Wave guitar players just kind of chunked along, concentrating more on writing songs than arpeggiated leads or finger-tapping 'til they got to Eddie Van Heaven. Maybe I was slumming it as a guitar player, but it didn't matter. Me and the guys were gonna get laughed at and ridiculed no matter what we did.

We played a few shows downtown, and then, in Grade Thirteen, we were asked to play one of our school dances. The invitation took us by surprise because we didn't think that anyone cared or was paying any attention to us at all short of calling out "freak!" or "weirdo!" in the hallway. I guess the teachers noticed, though, because it was one of them and a few kids from student council who asked us to play. We'd played at one high school dance before, in Scarborough – miles from where we lived on the other side of Toronto – and passed out 45s after our set; as we crossed the dark dance floor, kids winged the platters at our heads. At our school we feared the worst. But as soon as we started playing, the other kids could see that we weren't bad, so they dropped the bull-shit and started dancing. It was total *Cotton Candy*, Disney shit, Gord; a real triumph. We graduated a few months later, and while high school still more or less sucked, at least we went out on top.

A lot of kids rebel in high school, and playing in a New Wave band was our rebellion. Some kids get into drugs or black magic or vampires or knives or bisexuality or conservativism or veganism or paganism or plush toys or subway tagging or German theatre or wild haircuts or cell-porn or protesting or hacking computers or blow jobs or getting pregnant. Kids growing up in the twenty-first century have lots of ways to rebel, but the whole idea of rebellion becomes more predictable with each generation. If a kid doesn't rebel these days, parents get worried, but in the 1950s – which was the beginning of North American teenage rebellion, or at least the popularization or maybe the marketing of teenage rebellion – to be a rebel was to be truly bad, as opposed to the kids these days who go to the mall, get a twenty-dollar tattoo as a gesture of independence, and think they're Damian Abraham or Jenny Mechanic.

All of this brings me to what it is I think I know about what it was like for you as a musician in high school. First of all, you didn't like rock and roll. You once described it as sounding like "death after the high school prom," which is a pretty good line and which I think would be a good name for a grungecore band: Death After the High School Prom. Anyhow, what's interesting is that while most kids would have found the music of Chuck Berry and Elvis and Little Richard and Carl Perkins to be a means of rebellion and liberation, instead you *pffffted* and yawned: there was nothing in it for you. Instead of forming a rock and roll band, you did two things, both of which were gestures of total squaredom (Death After the High School Prom's first album: *Gestures of Total Squaredom*). First, you joined the Society for the Promotion of Barber Shop Quartet Singing in America, Inc.

(you also joined the Collegiate Four, a local barbershop trio); and next, you bought a set of drums, wanting to learn how to play jazz. Whatever was cool, you did the opposite. And the more popular rock and roll became, the harder you worked at not having to play it. I won't tell you who told me, Gord, but there were a lot of rock and roll musicians in the area who were cheesed at you, because whenever they went to book a gig, they discovered that you'd already booked one for yourself. It was as if you were single-handedly trying to prevent the evolution of rock and roll in your town. One can't help but be impressed by the tirelessness of your endeavour, but it's all I can do to not ask why it was so important to you. That, and why anyone in their right mind would ever want to sing barbershop.

So, you embraced the uncool. And that's probably what makes you cool. But here's something I don't understand. In your high school yearbook, where you were asked to fill in the section marked "Pet Peeves," you wrote "Squares." But you were a total square. Were you being funny and ironic? Or were you just confused? I've known a lot of really great musicians who floated savant-like through the world without any concept of cool or otherwise, but this can't apply to your times. It was the fifties. Cool was all, cool was everything. Besides, just a few years later, you were playing Top Forty – rock and roll and pop – with your pal Whelan in the lodges and taverns of Ontario. By doing this, and by singing barbershop, maybe the message you were sending to people – to your friends, to your parents, to the world – was that you were

Gordon Lightfoot, and you didn't care. If no one in Orillia was singing jazz or show tunes or barbershop, you would. A few years later, no one in Canada was singing about Canada, either, but you were. And in the sixties, when folk music was going electric, you stayed away from drums and fuzz guitar like they were hep A and B. You played at Newport right before Dylan's show, the one where he went electric. You were introduced before your set by Peter, Paul, and Mary – I imagine them sandaled in flowered caftans, arms bouqueted with tin whistles and recorders, one of them snuggling an autoharp – but not many people remember it because of Dylan's performance, which left his long-time fans in tatters, many of them demanding an apology from their young bard. Afterwards, folkies let their autoharps *sproing* against the floor, their herbal tea oil-lamped utopia of cartoon dragons and Castenedian poetry ground under by The Band's muddy colossus and Dylan's electric depravity. No one is sure how you felt, but in the following six to eight months, while every Tunesman or Merry Wanderer or Laughing Dolphin Quintet was tacking music shops with ads looking for bassists and drummers, you quietly returned home to work on your songs. Maybe it was an act of defiance, maybe not. If Dylan's new sound continued to vibrate like that of an insane laughing ghoul in the ear chambers of those who'd heard it, you rejected any impulse to change. Dylan's new sound might have begat the Mamas and the Papas – just saying their name troubles my digestion, Gord – but you went out and hired two accomplished and creative sidemen: Red Shea and John Southlick. As it turned out, it was just enough change.

Asked to fill out the section of your yearbook marked "Probable Destination," you wrote: "Diaper washer at Wagg's." Here, I think you were being funny. Still, what I think you were really saying was: "I am Gordon Lightfoot. I will do whatever the fuck I want and no one is going to tell me otherwise."

O n Wednesday, the skies continued to bubble and hiss, foam and spit. The world was in vertical tumult, top to bottom, clouds to dirt. That morning, two Starfighter jets collided in mid-air over Brussels. The planes were torn apart, one crashing into a house and the other nose-diving hard into a farmer's field. Remarkably, both pilots bailed to safety and no one was seriously injured. The disaster happened suddenly, like the batting of a dragonfly's wings, while in the skies above the U.S.A., the drama was protracted, and, in the end, much less miraculous.

It was mostly Melvin Fisher's fault. His plan was supposed to work, and, for a moment, it had. But then bad shit happened; bad shit that you don't want, that you don't need, especially when there's already a lot of bad shit going on. Melvin was a house painter and he needed money. He was divorced, with six children, and he had debts. Bad debts. He also had charges pending in Texas — swindling charges, the lowest kind – and no prospects for employment, at least not in Norman, Oklahoma. He hated painting houses. He hated fancying up big homes for wealthy men who called the crew "ladies" and who wanted him to know just how bad he was getting reamed having hired such wrinkle-assed hippies and losers. Melvin's wife had taken him to the cleaners in divorce court. The judge was a woman, so you know how that went. Melvin thought he would get money doing what a lot of other people had done, even though it had hardly ever worked. D.B. Cooper had done it, then disappeared. A few months later, Palestinian terrorists did it at the Munich Olympics, then flew to freedom. Maybe it was the sense of adventure that captured his imagination. Maybe it was the chance to show his ex-wife that he could assume responsibility once and for all. Or maybe it was the power that comes with holding a dozen strangers' lives in your hands and getting them back to earth no worse for wear. He wouldn't use bullets. That would be wrong. Jesus Christ, I'm no maniac, he thought to himself. I'm no killer.

The events of Wednesday night were also Michael Green and Lulseged Tesfa's fault, although Green and Tesfa treated their passengers much worse. If Melvin showed remorse after everything went wrong – sobbing uncontrollably in the judge's chambers and excusing himself every ten minutes to vomit once the reality set in that he would be spending the rest of his life trying to not get stabbed or ass-fucked in prison – Green and Tesfa were unrepentant. They were thugs and they knew what they were walking into. While Melvin brandished an un-loaded gun which he eventually surrendered to a stewardess,

Green and Tesfa pistol-whipped and shattered the pelvis of the National Airlines jet's co-pilot. They also shot the flight engineer, Gerald Beaver, before shutting off the lights in the cabin, cutting the air conditioning, and demanding that the plane be kept in the air interminably.

It was the first time in United States' history that two hijackings happened on the same day. The ransom demands were oddly similar – Melvin Fisher asked for $550,000; Green and Tesfa, $600,000 – but, otherwise, the two episodes were very different. Melvin's aerospace siege was over before it started. He'd lost the stomach for what he was doing pretty soon after the American Airlines plane took off, but tried seeing the plan through in an effort to prove something to himself, although damned if he knew what that was. His original idea was to fly from Oklahoma City to Fort Worth, get the cash and a parachute, and then jump to wherever the wind blew him. Melvin liked the randomness of the notion, as if the current would carry him into a fissure leading to some lost city of sleep, and where, even though he had all of the money, none of that would matter down there. But a storm raged across the south and the plane had to be diverted home. At first, Melvin thought it was a ploy, but the skies outside told a different story. Upon landing, authorities brought him a bag of money and a parachute, but this was only after Melvin agreed to release all fifty-seven passengers, as well as three stewardesses. Privately, he was relieved that the civilians were gone. If something happened later, fewer innocent lives would be lost. The pilot and flight engineer remained aboard, as well a stewardess, whom Melvin held hostage. She seemed like a nice person.

Green and Tesfa, on the other hand, kept their passengers hostage for nine hours in the air without AC or electricity. People fainted. Others screamed and called out to their captors. The 727 circled above the Philadelphia airport as the hijackers negotiated with FBI agents on the ground, landing only after the plane's fuel dropped too low to continue. Once on the tarmac, the pilot escaped through a window. All 113 passengers were released and the hijackers were transferred, along with four stewardesses, the co-pilot, and the flight engineer, to another aircraft, which, according to the Associated Press, "flew over Dallas, then Houston, then swung south over the Gulf of Mexico, eventually landing at Lake Jackson." One of the stewardesses fled from the plane, and then Green and Tesfa, despite having been given their ransom, surrendered; bond would later be set at one million dollars each. Hanging in the clouds, Melvin Fisher counted his money in the cockpit of the 727. When he got to the bottom of the bag, he saw that his hands were stained purple from the marked bills, which amounted to less than half of what he'd demanded: $200,000. Melvin asked the nice flight attendant if she wouldn't mind opening the rear door of the plane so he might jump out. Certainly, she might have said, twirling on her heels. Reports confirm that Fisher had the plane circle for two more hours as he saddled his parachute and worked up the courage to fall to earth. But he couldn't. Instead, he told the pilot to land, and the next thing he knew he was bawling into the flat of his hands as the charges were read from the bench. In the end, it's what people had always said about him: even with a weapon, the guy couldn't fight his way out of a paper bag.

Pioneer 10 kept moving, plutonium-powered and edging towards Jupiter. Scientists drank coffee and tracked it daily, then hourly, then in ten-minute segments, still hopeful that something so relatively small could avoid being destroyed by things forty times its size and hurtling at unknowable speeds. Months before its launch, NASA had crafted two gold-anodized aluminum plaques designed by Carl Sagan, Linda Sagan, and Frank Drake, which they attached to the spacecraft's bus. According to William E. Burrows, author of *This New Ocean,* each plaque showed "Earth's place in the solar system from which it came; a silhouette of the vehicle itself; when it was launched; a diagram representing fourteen pulsars that were arranged to show a scientifically literate being where the home star of this system was located; and a naked man and a woman. The man's right hand," wrote Burrows, "was raised as a sign of peace. The woman stood passively beside him." The writer recalls that "print and television media were confounded by the problem of showing naked people to American families" and that "the *Chicago Sun-Times* reacted by airbrushing out the couple's genitals and her breasts. Outraged feminists complained that the woman was placed slightly behind the man, did not have a hand up, and looked at him with apparent adoration that they insisted amounted to submission. The message that the male-dominated, macho NASA wanted to send to the farthest reaches of the universe, the angry women charged, was that their own sex was subservient." Burrows concludes that "the uproar over the plaque said as much about life on Earth as what it depicted," but, as the small vessel sailed towards its target, NASA could not have cared less about social or political protocol. This wasn't about politics, or gender, they said. It was about space. It was about humanity. It was about the universe. More coffee.

Millions of miles beneath the tiny chugging spacecraft, David McTaggart rubbed his beard while floating alone in the earth's soup, waiting for it all to go to hell. While he did this, he had an idea: he would rename the *Vega*. It would now be called *Greenpeace III* – after that new environmental group they'd started back home – and as the boat swished across the blue-green waters towards the French South Pacific, 125 miles east of the Cook Islands, McTaggart finally felt like he was part of something big, something that, one day, would swallow the world's attention. The captain sent a message to Radio Rarotonga: he had reached the nuclear test zone, just beyond the Moruroa Atoll. If they were going to blow shit up, he said, they would blow him up, too. The boat rocked softly. Its captain sat and waited for a response.

———

On Wednesday, police and soldiers scoured the fields and ditches around Kingston with dogs and guns and netting while the escaped convicts tried to make themselves invisible. One of them, Thomas Smith, curled up between two trees and dreamed of smoking. Smith loved to smoke. He loved the sweet, hot burn of the tobacco against the cool of his throat and how the nicotine reached his bloodstream as if it were swinging from a rope wearing a broad feathered hat and boots, a sword swishing through the air. He loved how the buzz tingled his shoulders and the base of his neck and the way the cylinder sat perfectly weighted between his fingers. He loved the idea of smoke as food and smoking as activity, and it's all he could think of as he hid in the nettled and rough bush outside of Napanee. He was free, and while freedom for some convicts meant easy pussy and fast cars and *Playboys* and buckets of booze and the warmth of sons and daughters and Mom's food cooked all day then served with a bottle of beer, cooler ice sliding down its neck as it warmed in their hands, for Smith, it meant smokes burned one after another, thinking about something then nothing then something then nothing again. He could bear it no longer. Sunny Day's Smoke and Gift was just on the other side of the bridge, its yellow sign visible from where the fugitive crouched. He gathered himself in his filthy prison greys and approached the front window crowded with Spiderman dolls and black joke gum and Kingston Canadians pennants and lava lamps and Apollo 11 modelling kits and a bucket of street-hockey blades and a slouch-shouldered and slowly deflating Bozo the clown sagging at the centre of the busy mess of kitsch. Smith opened the door, a tiny bell dinging below the frame. He asked for du Mauriers. Three packs. The old man behind the counter looked at Smith, then looked out the window before asking: "Three? Not four?" "Three," said Smith, before reconsidering. "No. Okay, four." "How about a carton?" asked the old man. Smith said no, he'd buy a carton later. The old man checked his stock then said that he'd have to retrieve a new carton that he kept at the back of the store. "No problem, take your time." Smith felt good. The old man hadn't even noticed what he was wearing. He hadn't smelled him; hadn't sized him up. Then again, he was pretty old. The man returned, holding three decks of du Maurier red. He stacked them on the counter. The door opened and the bell rang a second time. After apprehending Smith, Constable Goyer went through the details of his arrest before telling the writer from the *Star*, "You know, what caught that guy was his yearning for cigarettes."

At a reception at the Sutton Place Hotel in Toronto on Wednesday, it was made official: Canada would put its reputation as the world's greatest hockey nation on the line in an eight-game "Summit" series against a team from the Soviet Union. The announcement was made to the sound of Peter Appleyard playing his mallets while Ginni Grant (of the Phil Nimmons band) sang the new Team Canada song ("Team Canada, we're with you all the way!"), which the *Toronto Star* described as "folk rock." They also wrote that the "food, shrimps, scallops, and egg rolls were in abundant supply, and the models were more delicious than the food." As the names of the players were read, Harry Sinden drank his Molson Extra Old Stock and watched what looked like a goddamned fashion show on the goddamned Sutton Place hotel stage as two dozen grown men – hockey players, professionals, all of them – walked up there laughing and smiling in their white ties and plaid jackets while the goddamned photographers asked them to pose like goddamned fags in a goddamned fag parade. Harry had picked his players carefully for the series and the only thing that the goddamned writers wanted to talk about was Bobby Hull – Hull this; Hull that – and whether they were going to let him play, even though he'd named him to the god- damned team, which is what Harry said he would do all along. Sinden told Proudfoot, "We strove for balance; offense and defence; finesse and aggressiveness." And while the goddamned experts wondered why this player or that player wasn't named – there were no Penguins, no Kings, no Seals, and no Blues on the team – he could have named thirty-five other players and still, it wouldn't be easy beating the goddamned Russians because, sure, they were strange and their equipment was shit and they had weird names and flowerpot helmets and they came from a dark and horrible place far, far away, but, jeezus, have you seen them goddamned skate? After the introduc- tion, models wearing Team Canada sweaters and black mini- skirts worked the room, serving beer and champagne, but Harry couldn't even enjoy that. They were playing against Russia, and then they were going to Russia. He'd named Bobby

Hull, but now, the goddamned top brass that ran Hockey Canada were saying that, maybe, maybe, he wouldn't be allowed to go. Clarence Campbell and the goddamned NHL owners were behind it. They didn't want to give that new league, the WHA, anything to run with. They didn't want to be seen including any of its stars, even if it meant keeping the great Hull off the team. Harry drained his stubby. Politics. Owners. Goddamned Hull and his goddamned new contract with the goddamned WHA. Who's idea was it for him to coach this goddamned team anyway?

The French were furious. They'd spent months pushing the money through the system before rigging the detonators, clearing the atoll as best they could, and setting everything into place that would properly measure the effects of their blasts. Because that little Canadian shit McTaggart was where he was – downwind yet anchored, according to the official boundaries of international waters – he would be torn apart by the menacing Day-Glo of the enormous nuclear blast. The only way the tests could continue was if McTaggart and his Greenpeace vessel were removed. The French set about to do this.

truman capote was supposed to write about the tour for rolling stone and he brought a princess with him so how bad could it be but after awhile the little squeaky-voiced faggot had started hanging around backstage stealing all of the heat and jagger couldn't bear it anymore especially after the writer called him "as sexy as a pissing toad" and other things that made him seem smarter and more clever than mick and let's face it he was. besides it wasn't about books or words or magazine or tight-assed new york writers fuck no it was about rock and roll the beast spewing out whatever black shit was inside it all over america painting the place riot red and puke green and acapulco gold. so keith smeared the queer's door with ketchup shouting at him and calling him an old queen but the writer's heart wasn't in it anyway so it was so long gaylord thanks for nothing and besides it's wednesday so it must be indianapolis in a fucking convention centre of all places – jeezus – and last night keith's friend flex got the shit kicked out of him so bad by one of the bodyguards that he shit himself and now flex is off the tour and keith can't stand it so he reams out willie who is loading luggage on to the plane and who everybody likes but it's cobo hall tomorrow and things have to be cool because you know, sure, it can go off the rails in indy or ohio or wherever but when it all comes down to it, man, you don't fuck with detroit.

After *kachunking* an ad for next Tuesday's Rare Earth concert into the cart machine, someone named either Jungle Johnny or Cool Mo or Dave the Dragon or Electric Earl spent the better part of Wednesday afternoon spinning around in his chair to face a wooden rack in which the Top Forty singles of July 10, 1972, were hanging on dowels. Passing their hands

over the records as if working a Ouija board, the deejays pon-
dered whether to play "Layla" or "Lean on Me" or "Where Is
the Love?" or "Long Cool Woman (In a Black Dress)" by The
Hollies, the catchy T. Rex rip-job that was fast climbing the
charts. "Rocket Man" was there, too, and so was "Bad Side of
the Moon" by April Wine. The rest of the chart was largely
filled out by Canadian performers who weren't stars then, and
never might be: Doctor Music, Tommy Graham, A Foot in
Cold Water, Brave Belt, and Pagliaro, all of whom had reaped
the benefits of Trudeau's new bill, the Maple Law, which
forced Johnny and Mo and Dave and Earl to play Canadian
records, although, in the beginning, they were happy to do
this. The deejays made gig announcements, too: *Hey friends!*
Remember to catch Johnnie Johnson and his Shamrocks playing all
week long at the Town and Country Palace! or *Listen up fuzzlovers*
and psychedelios! How about that CNE Grandstand lineup this year
featuring The Guess Who with John Kay and The Stampeders rocking
the midway bowl?! or *Unsheath thy ears, remove thy hats, and prepare*
thy dialing fingers, celestial ones, for the Bob Marley and Genesis
ticket giveaways are forthcoming!! One of the gigs they wouldn't
have announced was a show by a newish local hard-rock band,
Rush, taking place at Toronto's Mental Health facility. The
band was consigned to play the gig after their first drummer,
John Rutsey, questioned the ethics of the musicians' union.
The union responded by forcing Rush to play a so-called trust-
fund gig at the insane asylum. According to crew member Ian
Grandy: "They took us to these ten-foot high barricaded doors.
[We knocked on the door] and a guy who looked like half of

his head had been melted tried to get out before being tackled to the ground. The crowd for the show was sixty people, including one guy who thought he was Elvis. They put seven old ladies right in front of the P.A. speakers. They sat there unblinking and catatonic." Geddy Lee, for his part, remembers another detail. "One of the inmates tried escaping with us during load out."

In between choosing records from the singles chart, as well as playing Pink Floyd, Steely Dan, and Led Zeppelin album sides, the deejays talked film, too, or least about movies that had some kind of musical connection: Jimmy Cliff's West Indian epic, *The Harder They Come,* with its groundbreaking soundtrack that introduced people to reggae artists not named Bob Marley; Gordon Parks' *Superfly,* whose Curtis Mayfield-written theme song had infused summer radio; *Fritz the Cat,* the first animated movie to receive an X-rating; *Lady Sings the Blues,* the story of Billie Holiday starring Diana Ross; and *Sounder,* whose cast included a dust-swept and dobro-playing Taj Mahal. They might have talked about 1972's other cinematic moments, too: Ned Beatty's feral turn in *Deliverance;* Shelley Winter's dog-paddle for daylight in *The Poseidon Adventure;* Tarkovsky's space-epic, *Solaris;* Woody Allen being chased around by an enormous breast in *Everything You Always Wanted to Know About Sex (But Were Afraid to Ask);* Joel Grey's transexual character in *Cabaret; Ben,* starring Michael Jackson and thousands of rats; *Boxcar Bertha,* Martin Scorsese's first film; two *Carry On* films, both of which played at my local movie theatre (I remember the decolletage of the women on the movie posters); *Pink Flamingos,* with Divine; *Kansas City Bomber,* with Raquel Welch as a roller-derby Amazon; and two hugely revolutionary films: *Deep Throat* with Linda Lovelace and Coppola's *The Godfather,* which dominated that year's Academy Awards.

The movie I remember most from 1972 is the romantic comedy *What's Up, Doc?* directed by Peter Bogdanovich with Ryan O'Neal and Barbra Streisand. I remember it because it was the first mature film I'd ever seen. There were no animated woodchucks or caped superheroes or *Old Yeller* animals in it; just caper laughs and mild sexual innuendo that passed my parents' test. I was nine years old and I would have gone to either the Westwood or Albion Mall cinemas, whose lobbies were dressed in seventies gold-and-brown curtains with red velvet walls. I remember the sugary darkness of the snack counter's Coke, and popcorn that snapped when cracked between my teeth. While going to the movies in 1972 wasn't that different from going to them today – there were trailers, torn tickets, dating couples, lonesome seniors, stuck-butter floors, and darkness – we were at least spared the torture of endless, pre-feature commercials. And there was smoking. Everywhere, smoking.

Despite these myriad entertainments, on Wednesday, rock critic and journalist Peter Goddard sat in the Queen's Quay offices of the *Toronto Star* looking to the weekend: two Stones shows as well as Mariposa, all of which he was required to cover. Before writing about rock and roll for a living, Goddard had spent time playing in bands up and down Yonge Street, "an old-style, Ray Charles-influenced two-handed piano player," he remembered. "I wasn't bad, just not really into the life. There were others out there – like Doug Riley – who were really terrific, so I headed to music school at U of T, where I did some composing, mostly electronic music. My name is actually on *Odd Balls,* a short film featuring that great leading man, novelist Robertson Davies."

In Goddard's opinion, Mariposa '72 wasn't regarded as a significant event until after the fact. "Actually, it wasn't until I sat down to write about the event that I realized what had just happened," he said. Bruce Cole, who was hired to photograph the weekend, echoed these words: "We didn't realize history was in the making until it had been made."

Goddard believes that the festival would have had greater immediate significance had it not come just a few years after the events of September 13, 1969, at Varsity Stadium, after which, he said, Flower Power was left bloodied and lifeless. There, John Lennon and his new wife, the small and enigmatic Yoko Ono, debuted their new group, the Plastic Ono Band. The concert – called the Toronto Rock and Roll Revival – represented the de facto end of the most beloved group in music history and marked the first time that any Beatle had ever performed solo. It also established Toronto as a city where remarkable events in music could, and would, take place.

The festival was produced by John Brower and Kenny Walker, who'd promoted another mega-show – the two-day Toronto Pop Festival – just a few months earlier. Because of poor early ticket sales, Brower and Walker lost the support of their two main backers – department store heirs George and

Thor Eaton — and the Revival was almost cancelled. But California garage-rock impresario and producer Kim Fowley, who was in Toronto along with announcer and Sunset Strip personality Rodney Bingenheimer to promote the event, suggested that Brower invite John and Yoko to emcee the festival as a way of igniting people's interest. Given Lennon's affection for the early days of rock and roll — Chuck Berry, Little Richard, and Gene Vincent were all booked to perform — it wasn't the most outrageous idea, and, as Goddard recalls, "those were the days when you could actually call up a rock star and get through to them on the phone, which is what Brower did. It's the same principle that applied to Mariposa, making it possible for all of the stars to show up and feel comfortable." After talking to Brower, Lennon asked if he could play instead. Brower immediately arranged travel for the band, which also included Eric Clapton, Alan White, and Klaus Voorman, as well as Beatles' road manager Mal Evans and Yoko's assistant, Anthony Fawcett. Media outlets in Toronto refused to believe that Lennon's appearance was anything more than a ruse until a Detroit radio personality, Russ Gibb, played bits from a telephone recording made of Fawcett confirming John and Yoko's flight agenda with Brower. On the morning of the concert, wire services reported that the musicians had boarded a flight from London to Toronto, at which point the remaining tickets sold. Not everyone who went to the show, however, used a ticket to get in. Musician Ken Whiteley, the eminent Toronto folk and gospel singer, who was eighteen years old at the time, "scaled a ladder that someone had put up outside the stadium.

I climbed over the top of the bleachers and sat wherever I could. When I entered the arena, Little Richard was up there playing on stage, and he was tearing the place apart. He was very competitive, and he killed. You could tell that it was his intention to blow John Lennon and his band off the stage."

Geddy Lee, who went to the show with John Rutsey, remembered that Lennon's appearance was a true surprise. Because of the nature of communication in 1969, you wouldn't have known about it had you not been listening to the radio that day. The same dynamic applied to what would happen a few years later at Mariposa: lacking BlackBerries or cellphones or other digital apparatuses, word of the surprise performers would have travelled via sightings and word of mouth, if it travelled at all. Geddy said that "all throughout the day, there were announcements from the stage of a very special guest. They were teasing us by not saying who it was, then they revealed that it was John Lennon with a supergroup. As the day turned to evening, they announced between every act that they had arrived at the airport; they were en route to the stadium, etc. They really hyped the crowd before, eventually, they took the stage."

If Mariposa would provide a kind of easy idyll where musicians and fans communed in an island setting, the Revival was staged at the simmering heart of the dirty city. At one point, a police cruiser was attacked and rocked by fifty kids, while, inside the stadium, fans staged garbage fights; others flipped out on acid and PCP. The show itself was a mixed bag. According to the *Star*'s Melinda McCracken, singer and guitarist Bo Diddley was dressed in a "dark red metallic suit" and ignited the crowd of 20,000 by "stomping around the stage" before ending his set by dropping to his knees and weeping. The Chicago Transit Authority played next, then gave way to the day's march of legends, which included a tired-looking and portly Gene Vincent, who was backed by the Alice Cooper Band and surrounded by Vagabond bikers standing arms crossed at the front of the stage. According to McCracken, Jerry Lee Lewis nearly destroyed his instrument by "jumping up and down on the grand piano," while, during Chuck Berry's set ("he possessed an aura of slick vulgarity," wrote McCracken) a group of fans tore off their clothes before being painted with mustard by Bingenheimer. Little Richard showed up accompanied by a big show band and wearing "a beautiful white suit covered in little one-inch mirrors." In Goddard's words, "Little Richard didn't care about the event being historic or anything. He just went out there and played. It was clear from the beginning that he wasn't about to be up-staged by anyone, especially not a Beatle."

Three Toronto musicians were part of Chuck Berry's backing band, among them Danny Taylor and Hugh Leggat of Nucleus, which became the foundation for Foot In Cold Water. Taylor and Leggat attended the show at the invitation of Brower, who managed Nucleus along with Shel Saffron, producer of the Amboy Dukes and others. Taylor remembered that "Shel asked us early in the day if we wanted to back up Chuck Berry, and we said, 'Yeah, sure, whatever.' We didn't think anything of it because it seemed like an insane idea.

Then, just before the show was supposed to start, he said, 'Okay, you're on in a few minutes.'" Leggat remembered that "the bass player who was supposed to play with Chuck was shaking because he didn't know the tunes. But no one did. Chuck didn't travel with a band; he just picked up musicians in whatever town he was playing. So I figured that, shit, you know, I didn't have anything to lose."

Leggat remembered the legendary guitarist turning away from the band on purpose so that they couldn't see his hands. "It was impossible to figure out what key he was in, and, at one point, I went over and I asked him. He held up his hands, stopped whatever song we were doing and told 20,000 people: 'The bass player here wants to know what key we're playing in!' He was toying with us. It wasn't until after about a half an hour into the show that he settled into playing some slow blues, and that's where it actually started to click. At one point, I looked over and there was my brother at the side of the stage. He was gesturing with his head, and standing beside him was Jim Morrison. My brother had this long wineskin with him and Jim asked for a drink. He drank it all and it spilled down the front of his T-shirt. The booze was laced with homemade meth and three kinds of acid, but Jim didn't seem to mind. He grabbed my brother and said, 'More! I want more!'"

Taylor remembers: "After the gig we were sitting around in the dressing room. Chuck said he was hungry and Hughie asked him if he'd ever had a Harvey's hamburger. 'What's that?' asked Chuck, and so Hugh told him. Chuck asked where he could get one, and we told him that there was a place across the street. So the two of us and Chuck Berry – who was still dressed in his stage clothes: a paisley vest and suit – crossed Bloor Street at St. George, where we stood in line and ordered burgers." Leggat recalls: "I remember the guy who was flipping the burgers asking Chuck if he wanted cheese on his. Chuck asked, 'What's that cost?' The guy told him, 'Five cents,' and he said, 'No way. I don't want no cheese.'"

"We were sitting backstage eating our burgers when, all of a sudden, this big British guy walked in," Taylor recalls. "I recognized him, but I didn't know from where. It was Mal Evans, the Beatles bodyguard and do-anything guy. All of a sudden, I heard screaming like I'd never heard before, and when the door opened, Eric Clapton and Klaus Voorman walked in, followed by John and Yoko. John was taking those long Groucho Marx strides and he said hello to Chuck. Chuck just looked at him and scowled. After awhile, he fucked off and never came back. He was always very bitter about Lennon and The Beatles. He thought they'd stolen his sound, stolen his music."

"After that," Leggat remembers, "Little Richard came in the room, shirtless and in tears. Little Richard was a strong man. He could pick up a table with his teeth, and he was in great shape. But he was crying, tears streaming down his face. He stood right beside me shouting to Lennon in a high, effeminate voice: 'Johnny Lennon! Johnny Lennon! I know you love me because you sing all my stuff; all of the *woo hoo!* all that! Johnny Lennon, why aren't I going on last? Why, Johnny, why?' He was just freaking out on him." Leggat could see that Lennon was cornered, and that he didn't know what to do. Eventually, he got up and left. A little while later, Mal Evans came back and said to Little Richard: 'Mr. Lennon wants you to know that, in his opinion, sir, you are indeed the King of Rock and Roll.' That turned out to be enough to calm him down."

The Plastic Ono Band had been escorted to Varsity Stadium from the airport by The Vagabonds, whose eighty members rode forty in the front and forty in the back, guiding the motorcade as it wound down Bloor Street towards the stadium. Music writer Ritchie Yorke wrote, "John was extremely nervous and jet-lagged. He hadn't been onstage in three years. He said, 'Imagine if you were in The Beatles from the beginning, and you were never in any other band? Then all of a sudden you're going onstage with this group who've never played live together. We formed on the plane coming over, and now we were going to play in front of 20,000 people.'"

Before they went on, host Kim Fowley asked the crowd to light matches or wave lighters as a means of easing John Lennon's uncertainty and stage fright, in the process establishing what is now a long-standing rock and roll concert tradition. Peter Goddard remembered that "people seemed very aware that rock and roll history was about to unfold. There was excitement and expectation and it was a true revelation. At that time, no one really knew who Yoko was or what she was about. The first time anyone saw her, she was crawling out of a white canvas bag, screaming like a maniac." Bruce Cockburn, who was the subject of a failed fan petition to get him on the bill, said, "What Yoko did on stage with the Plastic Ono Band is a lot cooler when you consider it in retrospect.

At the time, people weren't exposed to performance art, but knowing what we know now, we can understand her appearance as being more than just the ravings of a lunatic." Geddy Lee recalls: "They played some old rock and roll classics – 'Blue Suede Shoes' and 'Money' – and they also played 'Cold Turkey,' which had never been performed before. For the most part, Yoko was in a big white canvas bag on the stage beside John, making cat-like noises. Most of the crowd around us were laughing and not impressed. It did not go over very well at all, but we were so in awe of Lennon's presence – Clapton, too – that she was quickly forgotten. I remember that, after they played their last song, they left the stage with their guitars leaning on their amps and feeding back. It was very surreal and the only experience I had ever had watching one of the Fab Four in concert. The Doors closed the show and were incredible. Really, I was just lucky to have been there."

Peter Goddard is less forgiving than either Bruce or Geddy. "Their set was awful," he said. "The band was great, but Yoko ruined the show. You could tell that Lennon wasn't right and that things were quite grim for him. Both he and Clapton were going through heroin withdrawal, so it couldn't have been easy being there. Fans hated it and people left. Still, Lennon credited that show with making him believe that he could do it on his own."

David Keshen, who was sitting few a feet away from the stage, said, "When Yoko came out of her bag, the look on Eric Clapton's face suggested that he just wanted to shrink away."

In his review of the show, the *Star*'s other music writer, Jack Batten, concurred: "It's hard not to conclude that John Lennon hasn't saddled himself with an awkward, demanding and difficult and weird partner – and co-leader – in his current musical enterprises. Miss Ono offered yet another glimpse of her excruciating vision [while] in the process driving the crowd insane with boredom." Once she emerged from her bag, Yoko performed twenty minutes of original material in which she stretched her "vocalese into endless tedium, full of cries from hell; piercing, evil shrieks, tiny sounds that reminded you of a fingernail scratching across a blackboard." While all of this was happening, Batten described Lennon standing around with his hands in his jacket pockets, and "looking like a man waiting for a very late streetcar."

After the show, John and Yoko faced reporters from a wooden bench in a small barren locker room in the recesses of the stadium, which smelled of gym socks and old drains. Yoko told the crowd, "We are interested in exploring new sounds. John and I are upset that we missed the whole Rock and Roll Revival, not seeing all of the performers who influenced The Beatles." As they slipped away into another room, someone asked Yoko what was next. She told them they were very tired and were going to bed.

The events of Mariposa '72 might never have transpired had the Varsity Stadium show not established Toronto as a place where the impossible was possible. The stars of Mariposa were likely drawn to the city for the same reasons as Lennon: the thriving music scene, entrepreneurs with access to the

Bruce Cockburn at Mariposa, 1972

new money of old families, a generation of kids hep to new
sounds and styles, and a lack of bullshit that tended to follow
these kinds of large-scale happenings around. Besides, unlike
L.A. or New York or London, the city was manageably-sized,
and, at the time, Canada, or at least Toronto, possessed both
a familiarity and northern exoticism. Remembering his visits
to the city from Ottawa, and occasional residence here in the
late sixties and early seventies, Bruce Cockburn recalls that
Toronto was an interesting place because "there was a kind
of tension between this great music scene with these really
great people on one end, and the big, bad city on the other.
Everyone makes a point that Toronto is such a clean city, but

I'd come home and wash my hands and the sink would turn black, as if I'd just cleaned dirt from my hands. On top of that, you had very sleazy elements — Yonge Street, in particular — going against old Victorian traditions where stores closed on Sundays and the liquor laws were archaic. It was a city of opposites. Every day, I'd leave my house on Augusta Street across from a Polish butcher that always had a pig's head hanging in the window, then go out and hear these remarkable musicians. At the time, the city was at a crossroads. The artists and their nightlife had a real impact on how it changed."

Toronto's reputation as a musical centre had been established years earlier through a gig map that attracted American blues and jazz musicians who were embraced by Toronto even while remaining unbookable in many parts of their own country. And because of the Commonwealth, British bands found a friendliness and commonality in the city, resulting in a lot of first-generation Toronto bands getting exposed to music that the rest of the continent was not. Musician Sebastian Angello — who played with Leggat and Taylor in one of the city's first hit bands, The Lords of London, whose single, "Cornflakes and Ice Cream, " was the first number-one record by a Canadian band — was a veteran of countless recordings and shows before he was twenty. His extracurricular life eclipsed anything that happened to him at high school, and he lived the kind of life at sixteen that his grey-suited Latin teachers or work-clothed shop instructors could only dream about. Their appearance at the CHUM stage just inside the Princes'

Gates during the 1967 CNE caused a riot that had to be quelled by police on horseback. By night, he was rock and roll girl candy, and by day, he was at his desk at school, studying Latin, science, and algebra.

Sebastian also played in a country band at the Edison Hotel on Yonge Street, but because he was underage, he wasn't allowed to stay after he performed. He used to creep upstairs to Steele's Tavern, where in the mid 1960s Lightfoot played every night. The doorman let him hang out near the entrance listening to the singer's low, resonant tenor as it drifted through the door, passing over him before it got lost in the steel wool of city traffic and people stamping down the busy sidewalks. He'd get home late, sleep later, and get up and do it all again.

The Lords of London were one of the city's busiest musical concerns. They were the opening band of choice for famous touring acts, and, within a few days of each other in 1969, they opened for both Jimi Hendrix and the Mothers of Invention. Angello remembers: "When Hendrix showed up at the Gardens, we were smoking a joint. He asked if he could have some and we said, sure, but he pretty much bogarted it. He'd just come across the border and was jonesing. The band hadn't been able to bring anything across, for obvious reasons, so the poor guy was desperate. But he seemed like a nice guy, either way. That night, I took his drummer, Mitch Mitchell, down to Yorkville after the show. We partied, had a good time, then, around three o'clock in the morning, he told me that he was hungry. I broke the news that there wasn't really anywhere to eat – back then, there were no twenty-four-hour restaurants in Toronto – so, I said, 'Hey, let's just go to my folks' place. I'm sure that my mom will fix us something.' So that's what we did. My mom got up and she made us this big pasta meal in the middle of the night: me, my buddies, and Hendrix's drummer sitting around eating. It was delicious. Before he died, I got an email from him telling me that, while there were a lot of things about touring with Hendrix that he didn't remember, this was something that he did. He remembered that night, and he remembered my mom's pasta."

The Lords of London were only one of countless bands playing in the city. The Kensington Market and The Ugly Ducklings were two other marquee rock acts who possessed a soulful rage and determined musicianship, and whose legions of followers were the first crowds attracted to, and crazy for, local rock and roll. Then there were The Paupers. When people talk about The Paupers, they pause before trying to describe the band's sound, then end up explaining that what they've said isn't nearly enough. The impressions come in flashes: early electronic treatments and sound waves snaking through the tumult of a wildly thundering band squeezed onto one of Yorkville's matchbox stages; a bass player, Denny Gerrard, whose solos were so intense and complicated that his fingers bled afterwards, and whom Geddy Lee cites as his first musical hero; songs that were epic and brave without being pretentious or silly; televisions that were occasionally destroyed at the end of sets; and a lead singer, Adam Mitchell, who was as poetic as he was defiant, and who was purportedly a friend of Dylan's, which, for some, validates the importance of the singer and his band. *The Village Voice*'s Richard Goldstein wrote, "The Paupers make impossible sounds with their instruments, and it is all there, right before you, real." But understanding the band's greatness is a little like peering into an overgrown and untended vista. Fans admit that their records never properly captured the band's raw power, and so we are left with the mere outline of a story, and only the studiofied image of one of Canada's wildest, most expressive, and chimeric bands.

The Paupers were managed by Bernie Finkelstein. By 1972, Bernie, in his words, had already gone through five or six careers working with the band. He flew to New York City when he was nineteen – the first time he was ever on a plane – to try and get a record contract for The Paupers with Jerry Schoenbaum of MGM and Verve Forecast: a singles deal, which, says Finkelstein, took two hours to sign. It was 1966. Bernie recalls: "Jerry set up a meeting between me and Howard Solomon of the Cafe Au Go Go on Bleecker Street, one of the happening clubs at the time. When I went to see Howard, he brought out this big book – a gig calendar – and he said that he had the perfect show for us, opening for Ian and Sylvia, who were also from Toronto. I told him that that was fine, but when I looked at the book, I saw that the Jefferson Airplane were scheduled to play around the same time, about three months later. I asked about them, and Howard said, 'Sure, you can have that. It'll give you time to record your first single, and then you can come and play.' I hadn't heard the J.A., but I knew that they were a growing concern in San Francisco, and

Bernie Finkelstein, far right, with Dan Hill, second from the left

that there was a lot of buzz about them. I went out and bought one of their records, and called The Paupers over to listen to it. It was semi-awful, and we all thought that we could blow them off the stage. Then, a few weeks later, I heard one of their new songs on the radio and it sounded completely different. It was 'Somebody to Love'; a great record with the band's new singer. Turned out, I'd bought their first album, recorded before Grace Slick had joined the band. Still, we were confident. Songs like 'We are the Magic People' would blow people away, and when Denny Gerrard did his bass solos, people went out of their mind. I've matured enough to know that being good isn't the only thing that matters in the music business, but back then, when people said that you were good, it meant that you played well. Now, everybody plays well but few people are actually very good. That might just be an old cranky guy talking, but maybe not."

The Jefferson Airplane shows in New York represented the first time that the San Francisco movement had come east. The Paupers, who opened both nights, were met with a curious and excited audience ready to embrace the vanguard of psychedelia. Brian Epstein, Paul Simon, Linda Eastman — who would take the band's promo shots — and Albert Grossman were in the audience, and, reviewing their show, the *Village Voice* wrote that "last night, a fresh wind from the north blew into town." Finkelstein remembers: "The following day, Albert Grossman called me up and said that he wanted to meet me. At that time, there was no one more important in my life than Bob Dylan, and that his manager — Albert — was calling me up was beyond my wildest imagination. He was also Lightfoot's manager, and that made it even more unreal.

"Lightfoot is the single most important reason why I got into music. He was my first hero. As a person, he thrills me more than anyone because he stayed here, he lived here, and he was very accessible, in his own way. It was refreshing. Before Gordon, it seemed as if every musician came from either London or New York, or they were Frank Sinatra. After hearing his records on the radio, and learning that he lived where I lived, I went in search of him in a strange kind of way. I wanted to be where he was, which, at the time, was Yorkville. I wasn't a musician, but I knew that I wanted to be part of what he was doing, in whatever capacity. People like Gordon helped locate me, gave me a sense of place, which is hugely important to anyone trying to find their way.

"I ended up taking a cab to Albert's place in Chelsea. When I showed up, Sally Grossman — Albert's wife, and the woman on the cover of [Dylan's] *Bringing It All Back Home* — answered the door. For years, I'd been staring at that album cover, and there she was. I went inside, and got more stoned than I'd been in my entire life. And that's when Albert asked me to be his partner."

After his days with The Paupers, Finkelstein went on to manage two of Yorkville's newest stars, Murray McLauchlan and Bruce Cockburn. He also started True North Records, which helped give the record industry in Canada a domestic focus. For him, Mariposa '72 wasn't so much about the arrival of the surprise guests because, he said, "Bruce Cockburn was about to play his first sold-out show at Massey Hall, while Murray had a number-one record – 'The Farmer's Song' – on the Country, FM and Top Forty charts. It won five Junos that year. I'd set a goal for myself and for my artists and we were getting there. My world was circulating around them, not the performers who showed up on the island. I was thick-headed and I only wanted to go one way: up. I was not going back to sharing a flat in Yorkville. I was fucking going for it."

With so many homegrown stars making an impact in Canada and around the world – and with CanCon pushed to its full legislative tilt – Canadian music found itself in the summer of '72. "It was as if the country's music was maturing," recalls Roly Greenway. "Trudeau's government had brought in CanCon, and we jumped on it. People don't realize how hard it was before there was any action on the radio. People didn't embrace Canadian bands like they do now, and, as a result, you sometimes ended up playing the worst places, clubs where you had to puke and show your razor blade before you walked in. We would back up strippers for six nights a week. We were called The Ascots and we did covers. Once, we heard that Ronnie Hawkins was doing auditions to find a group of players to replace The Band, so we'd play until one a.m. in London, drive down to Hamilton, get there at three, rehearse or audition until seven, and then drive back to London and go to bed, which, sometimes, wasn't even a bed. It was a floor. After we got the gig, we were living above the Hawk's Nest – Ronnie's Yonge Street club – subsisting on hot dogs, one per day. Ronnie was cheap and he figured that if he starved us, we were his, which, more often than not, proved to be true because we did not want to go back to the strip clubs. Ronnie used to fine you five dollars for stepping on his mic cables. Once, we did two sold-out nights at the Fillmore East in NYC opening for Joe Cocker and The Stone Poneys, and he gave us twenty dollars each. We'd been living with his sister in Long Island, and he told us, 'Well, you know, I've got to pay my sister for all of the food she's been feeding you,' which were more hot dogs, and the occasional can of beans. That's why making it on our own was so huge for us. No one could have imagined the impact of a hit song, and what it would mean. I remember pulling up in the van in 1972 to a gig in Oshawa and seeing all of these people crowded around the sidewalk. I thought that there must have been some kind of horrible accident. But they were fans. They knew our song and were thrilled that we were there. I remember the look on everybody's faces. We were rock stars."

According to Finkelstein, it wasn't only CanCon that changed things in the seventies, but the lowering of the drinking age in 1971. "Drinking altered the tastes of the average kid in Toronto. It's one of the reasons why a band like Rush was able to find an audience. At that point, you had to be loud, but it's not like you could be message-heavy, either, because people were having too good a time drinking and having fun." As for the Maple Law, however, not everyone was a fan: Al Mair, Lightfoot's old manager, recalls: "Lightfoot, of course, was opposed to it because he didn't need it, and because he felt that it would threaten his domination of Canadian radio. I spoke at the public hearings in support of it, but not without a certain amount of consternation. I didn't tell Gord until after I'd done it because I knew that he wouldn't have approved."

If the summer of '72 represented a time when Canadian bands were reaping the benefits of a new musical enlightenment, it wasn't long after that the contradictions of CanCon were revealed like traplines in the melting snow. Society of Composers, Authors and Music Publishers of Canada associate and musician Peter Otis said that "after awhile, programmers got wise and played most of their CanCon at night. They buried it. And in a lot of ways, they still do. Most radio stations don't come near 33⅓ per cent. Programmers get called out, but, the truth is, nobody wants to be told what to play." Musician David Bradstreet remembered that "at first, it was a great breakthrough. A real celebration that people were finally getting noticed and making a living, a career, out of being a Canadian musician living in Canada. But when I got my A&M deal in 1977, I went across the country on a promo tour. Because of the Maple Law, people were being forced into accepting a diet of whatever record companies were putting out. One time, me and an A&R guy gave our new album to a radio programmer. He looked at it and immediately threw it on his desk, at which point it skittered across straight into the garbage can. While it was still skittering, I remember the programmer moaning aloud: 'Ah, fuck, not more CanCon!'"

LETTER IN WHICH YOU PLAY A RESORT AND WE MEET A VENTRILOQUIST

Hey, Gord. Here's another newspaper clipping. I made this one up, too:

ADVERTISEMENT FROM ORILLIA TIMES,

JUNE 7, 1956

Appearing all month, Monday to Friday in the Manitou Room of the Big Chief Lodge, will be the ventriloquism and all-round hilarity of Sully and Silas, stars of the 1954 Canadian National Exhibition and the Wayne and Shuster Comedy Hour. Next month we feature the musical stylings of local up-and-comers The Two-Timers, singing songs from Your Feel-Good Hit Parade. Every Wednesday's dinner special is roast beef and mash and every Friday is half-price cocktail hour in the lounge, featuring the piano tinklings of Ford Masters, straight from his engagement at the Elks in Atherly.

Here's one I did not make up. I took it straight from Collins' book:

> *(The manager) offered them a chance (to play), on one stipulation: that their music not interfere with the conversation or the card playing. He was not overly impressed with the duo. He thought that Whelan had the better voice of the two, and that, "they were never going to amount to anything anyway." Today, he makes that statement with a rueful grin. He paid the boys five dollars, split between them.*

And here's something that you said after you got famous:

> *"I wish I could go up to Orillia more often. It was a great place to grow up in. There was hiking, swimming, boating. It was close to a big resort area – Muskoka – and when I was about fourteen, someone would get the old man's car and we used to hold concerts up there and just sing for a couple of beers to the summer folks."*

So: you started gigging. But before we get into all of that, let me tell you something that my wife said. She said it because every time one of my books comes out, someone gets mad at me. The reason they get mad at me is because they read about themselves and they think, "No, man, that's not how it happened!" or "No, man, that's not what I said." During the writing of my last book, I decided not to include this one person for those very reasons, but he was still mad: "How come you took me out of your book?" But here's what my wife said: "I learned a long time ago that whenever I show up in one of your books, it's not me: it's a portrait of me. A reductionist portrait. I've decided not to take it too personally." That's maybe a long way around saying that, yes, I understand that of course things happened in your life between the time you sang at Massey Hall and the barbershop groups and what happens here. Collins talks about you being a delivery-truck driver at Wagg's and how your barbershop group, The Teen Timers, got booked to sing at a few local resorts and how they wrote positively about you in the *Toronto Telegram* and, as a result, you got an offer to go to New York, but you balked because "finishing [your] education was more important than going south." He also writes that you joined the school's glee club and dated a girl name Shauna Smith and sang in a high school production of *The Mikado*. But I'm not going to write about those things; they've been written before. Besides, Collins printed a picture of you as a teenager wearing makeup and dressed all pretty-like in a kimono. It's a small thing, I know, but notice that in this book, you only look grown-up and fucking cool. No naked baby pictures here. You're welcome.

So, you got a booking, a gig, at a place called the Big Chief Lodge, playing three 45s a night. Whelan's dad knew a guy who knew a guy who knew a guy. Doing a little free engine work was a reasonable enough price to pay to teach his son and his son's friend that the ropes were rough and made to bruise, and that, if logic prevailed, they'd understand once and for all that music belonged in a church or maybe an opera house in continental Europe, which Orillia wasn't, and of which it had none. But Whelan's dad hadn't factored in how proud you'd both feel leaving the house in the late afternoon carrying your guitar cases knowing that you weren't headed to choir practice or music class, but to work. You might have left the house feeling that your guitar was your shovel, your axe, your fishing pole, your scythe. Whelan threw the car in reverse and you were peeling out of there before you could know otherwise.

You renamed yourselves the Two-Timers. You played songs by the Everly Brothers and Harry Belafonte. I imagine the Big Chief soldiered by a resort staff in red vests and dark trousers, kids mostly your age but some dinosaurs too, who moved about the oak and chandeliered two-storey hotel carrying a net of fresh trout into the kitchen off a flatbed parked behind the building, at least when they weren't dragging hoovers and dustbins across the impeccable gold-flecked carpets cleaned twice a day or parading trays of silver-domed lunches up the stairs to industrialists, councilmen, or honeymooners drawn to the postcard idyll for which the lodge was famous. After absorbing the scene, you and Whelan might have walked through the portal doors of a place that might have been called the Manitou Room, where a dozen lunching couples – women in capris, men in cardigans, holding hands – sat watching a small, tired-eyed ventriloquist in a tilted black bowtie fisting an ugly puppet and making fun of Diefenbaker.

"So Silas, what do you think The Chief's next move will be?"

"From the icebox to the refrigerator, I figure!"

"I've heard that he hopes to extend diplomatic relations with China."

"Well, you know The Chief: anything for a dish of egg chow mein!"

Afterwards, the ventriloquist might have come into the small dressing room where you and Whelan were standing. If your first real adult musical experience was anything like mine, you would have been standing there, hands pressed in pockets and grinning, so happy and free to be on this perfect little piece of musical property, no matter how dank or small or shitty it was, at least compared to other places you'd come to know. The room was utility ugly, but it was yours; a pocket of quiet removed from the bustle of the hotel. The ventriloquist threw his puppet on the tattered backstage couch as if ridding his hand of some unwanted gunk. The puppet lay there with its arms flung open like a drunk starlet. Sully hiked up his trousers, pulled a flask from the pocket of his blazer, lit a Sweet Cap, drained the flask in one draw, and said, "Goddamned victims. Half of them don't know what they're in for. The other half know, sure, but they can't help themselves."

Although putting words in a made-up ventriloquist's mouth is one thing, Gord, putting words in yours and Whelan's is another thing. So try to not get mad at me for writing:

"Name's Whelan. This here's my friend, Gordon," your pal might have said, extending his hand.

"No offence, but I give a shit as much as that box of matches over there," said Sully, shooting his arm in the direction of the puppet.

"Gordon and I are playing here tonight. It's our first real gig," said Whelan.

"Well, in that case, know three things," said Sully. "One, the waitress with the big charlies has the clap. I should know because she got it from me. Two: don't trust the owner; he'll screw you eight ways to Sunday. And three: the cook horks in the chowder. Never order the chowder."

"Heck, we don't even like chowder," joked Whelan.

"What's the matter with this one?" asked Sully, pointing at you. "Doesn't this one talk?"

"No, I talk," you might have assured him.

"Apparently."

"We're all pretty new to this," said Whelan. "And if I might say, we're pretty darned excited."

Sully picked Silas up from the couch like a washerwoman grabbing a laundry rag. He drew a silk-lined box from under the couch and stuffed Silas in headfirst. Fighting the smoke that gathered about his eyes, Sully pinched the cigarette from between his teeth, exhaled with a grimace, then turned towards you and your friend.

"Well, you're not new anymore."

You and Whelan went out there and played. For me, Gord, my first gig was a thrilling and remarkable blur – a moment of glorious, if uncertain, fragments – and I wonder if yours was the same. After your set, you might have thought that people had listened to the songs, but you weren't sure. They'd eaten their food and applauded politely after every tune. Backstage, one of the waiters, a brush-cut kid who I'll call James

— he had a quick smile and ears like New England clams — came and asked what kind of reward you were after. Not understanding, you stared at him until he said, "Beer or whiskey. But not wine. You're not going to be like that, are you?"

"Either would be great," said Whelan, answering for both of you.

"Great. Beers and a bottle of C.C. for my newest favourite performers," he said. "I get off at ten. Meet me at the dock. No one will be out. The temperature drops below 70 and the victims hit the sheets faster than your uncle on Jane Wyman," he said.

Awhile later, you left the Manitou and walked out the back of the hotel to the end of a long wooden dock, where James was lying on his back looking up at the sky, which had melted purple, speckled with stars.

"You did a lot better than most of them," he said, sitting up to *pfftt* open three bottles of cold Pale Ale and pass them around. "Not a single complaint, which is pretty much how we measure things around here."

"People complain?" asked Whelan.

"Usually if it's too loud or if the musicians talk too much to the audience. Management doesn't want you to be much more than background music. You know, easy money and everything. Besides, those victims; all they want to do is eat their dinner and get back to fucking like monkeys."

"Sounds cool to me," said Whelan.

"Well, most of the performers who come through here learn how to cope, if you know what I mean," said James, drawing the twenty-sixer of C.C. from his bag and unscrewing the top.

"Sully doesn't seem to be coping so well," said Whelan. "That guy is some kind of weird."

"Still, he's a professional," he said, tugging on the whiskey and passing it around. "That's all management asks for. He does his show. He doesn't bother anyone. He's quiet. Although I'd like to turn that cornball dummy into firewood, given half the chance."

"Looks like Sully would do the same thing if it wasn't his meal ticket."

"Some meal. When he isn't working, the guy lives in his car. Never married. But he plays regular. That's all you can really hope for in this racket," said James.

"Seems kind of lame. Just wanting that," you said, speaking for the first time.

"Marcel Marceau has an opinion?" said James.

"Yeah. Sometimes," you said.

"Hey, a shtick is a shtick. I've seen lots of acts come through here. And what you guys need is a shtick. Ever think of incorporating comedy into your act?"

"No," said Whelan. "You think that would work in a hit parade kind of show?"

"It might, it might," said James, taking a pull from his beer. "Don't really think it's been done before."

"Songs about this town. That hasn't been done before, either, you know," you said, realizing while you said it that the idea of a rock and roll song about Orillia and the land was pretty absurd. At the time, rock and roll was all about cars, girls, spaceships, crazy new dances, and haircuts. The trees and the animals be damned.

"This town?" said James. "Why the hell would anyone want to write about this town?"

"I don't know," you said, retreating into your thoughts.

"This town," spat James. "We're stuck to it like flies to a gluestrip. Just hanging there, limb by limb."

"You can always write about the gluestrip," you said, knowing that, really, you could not.

You lay on your back swigging first from the beer, and then the whiskey (in his book, Collins suggests that it was during these gigs that you developed a taste for alcohol). You thought about what Sully was doing at this moment: sitting in the near-dark of his room as the TV painted his face in the radiant patchwork of whatever shitty program was shining through the glass. You thought about what it meant to become what he'd become and how you refused to be that not because of the loneliness and emptiness of the migrant entertainer's life, but because you couldn't live with yourself if you didn't follow your gut. What would it mean not to write about the way the forest darkened as the sun fell into the horizon as you trailed your father along a scrub path after a day of angling, walking back to the cottage where your uncles sat on lawn chairs drinking from mason jars with the kitchen light glowing behind them and the sound of women *chirupping* inside while a baseball game barked on the transistor? You became drawn so deeply into this memory that you didn't notice that James had taken out a tobacco pouch, slivered a cigarette paper from his pocket, and tapped a thread of crumbled green leaf across the crease.

"You guys hip to pot?"

You were about to tell him that, no, you were new to it all: to the sensation of being on your own playing music, to pot and booze, to people like Sully and people like James, and to the idea of writing about the gluestrip, and to the possibilities that once slept quietly in your dreams but now seemed suddenly alive. But you did not. Because the puppeteer was right: you weren't new anymore.

'72

THURSDAY, JULY 13TH

Buddy Smith, the fugitive pitcher, was starving. He chewed hay, he ate bugs. And then he met Teresa Miller. He'd been hiding out behind the barn shoeless and wearing his prison clothes. His arms and legs and neck had been savaged by mosquitoes while walking through the bush before finally reaching the farmhouse. When he first heard the footsteps coming, he was crouching, with hands balled into fists, waiting to pounce on whatever was approaching. But the kid was eleven. Wide-eyed. Mop-headed. Eye teeth loose in his head. In Paul Miller, Smith saw himself throwing a striped ball against the side of his boyhood home in Petrolia, imagining he was Whitey Ford or Bob Lemon or Early Wynn. Besides, the kid didn't really look scared so much as surprised. He called over his friend, Gerard, and they looked at the thirty-two-year-old escaped convict as if a new playmate had been delivered. When you're a kid living in the country, you're lucky if you have someone else to play with, and, in Buddy Smith, they thought that maybe they'd found their four-square third, a card partner, someone else with whom to play jacks or tiddly-winks. The kids said that they were hunting for robins' eggs. Did he want to join them? "He was very polite," Paul remembered. "He wanted to know the time. I told him that I didn't know and that I'd go up to the house and ask my mom."

Buddy rose from the deep grass at the side of the barn. He ran ahead of the kids and reached the house first. Teresa Miller recalls, "He entered the house and told me not to be scared and to not telephone the police. He said that he was hungry . . . so I made him some sandwiches." Smith devoured four of them – bologna and mustard – and, afterwards, Miller gave him an enormous slice of lemon meringue pie. The fugitive pitcher forked the dessert into his mouth while Miller told him about the roadblocks and the manhunt and the 150 troops who'd been called in from Ottawa. Sated and tired and filthy, Smith looked around the kitchen, drew in its scent and its warmth, and decided that the woman was right. Mrs. Miller phoned the police, then passed the receiver to the fugitive pitcher. "He asked the police to give him enough time to finish eating his lunch and have a shave (before they came to get him)," she said. Smith noticed that it had suddenly dawned on the boys that their visitor was one of the men who'd escaped from the nearby prison, at which point the pitcher told them not to be frightened. He wouldn't hurt them and, besides, he had sisters and a mother of his own. He sat there for a moment at the table, putting his arms behind his back and reclining in his chair. The legs creaked as it tipped back. It was a good sound.

After the television cameras had been cleared from the room, ice cubes found for Bobby Fischer's orange juice, and the International Chess Federation's seal covered so that the American would no longer be distracted or hounded or persecuted or whatever it was he said he was, the hall's attendants swept the game's ivory board clean with small, dark brushes; ceiling lamps were dimmed just so; and a handful of Russian officials stood whispering in their charge's ear as they waited for Fischer to enter the hall and begin the second game of the twenty-game match, which, of course, he did not. Fischer's one-hour time limit expired, forfeiting the game and giving Spassky a 2–0 lead. Privately, there were cheers among the Sovietskies, and the sense that the American player – like the U.S.A. and capitalism itself – would devour itself the way anything with too many choices and not enough discipline or dogma or direction would. In chessboard terms, one expert explained, "It was as if Fischer, were he a baseball player, had decided to go straight to the bottom of the ninth inning with the Russian ahead 5–0. Being down two games and coming back to win in chess is difficult at the best of times. Being down two games and coming back to win against a master like Spassky is nearly impossible." And since everything about chess was everything that Fischer appeared not to be – dispossessed of the composed and mechanical comportment required to play, as well as the stillness of thought needed to shuffle through the permutations of endless moves – the expert could have added that he was down two outs and hitting with a full count. It was raining; no, snowing; no, hailing. He was a strange man standing at home plate, totally alone.

Melvin Fisher was alone, too. While imprisoned, word reached him that transport authorities were meeting to discuss civil liberties and privacy laws and the comfort of their passengers in light of the recent hijacking scourge. After a few days, American Airlines announced that new security measures would be implemented, starting immediately. From now on, all future passengers would have their carry-on luggage – even purses and briefcases, rifle bags, fishing rods, and snooker-cue cases – checked by trained security personnel. There was outrage from consumer groups and people demanding protection from these potentially invasive procedures, but the new rules carried. Fly the friendly skies, said one airline. It was okay. Melvin Fisher would be behind bars forever.

David McTaggart saw them coming: enormous grey arrows cutting through the water. The noise was horrible: great machines gnashing their teeth, their engines roaring below the water, below the world. McTaggart pointed to his white flag, which must have looked silly to whoever was commanding the French minesweepers. They came faster, their great hulls bouncing *thwoam thwoam* as they hit the water. Behind him, one of McTaggart's new crew members barked into his radio, something like "Stoporyou'llfacetheconsequencesoftheworld'scourt!" But McTaggart didn't care. Either the *Vega* would hold its ground or he would be swimming in his heavy wet clothes in the South Pacific. It had to happen. It had to. Through the madness and the fear, it would be the first step towards making everything alright.

On Thursday, Colin Linden and his brother, Jay, went bowling at the Golden Mile Plaza. Colin remembered: "I was thinking ahead to Mariposa and what I could say in between songs. Using my best twelve-year-old Howlin' Wolf voice, I came up with: 'When I left New York two years ago, I was ten. Now I'm sixty-two. I grew fifty-two years in two years and if that ain't the blues, tell me what is.' I repeated it over and over to myself all the time. I knew I'd use it. I had a plan."

stevie couldn't figure out the stones but who could and even if you could would you really want to know what lay at the heart of this thing that spat in the face of fame and calm and rock and roll bliss and almost singlehandedly tore apart whatever remained of sixties cool and tie-dyed togetherness or as jack batten reviewing the cobo hall show said, "detroit trembled in anticipation of terrible things, just as every city was supposed to." one of the stones told a writer that stevie and his boys couldn't jam and they couldn't party but was it really so important so long as the shows were good every night but there's the rub: stevie was good, but were the stones? depends on who you ask. some say that they were a hot band molten to the core while others say that richards especially played like shit warmed-over and jagger tried to put it on his back but he couldn't and besides there was jealousy because stevie was a few months away from putting out talking book with the song superstition which he gave to jeff beck but beck fucked with it so stevie took it back and when his friends found out that he'd almost given it away they freaked because that song, man, it's so good, did he want to be on white radio so bad that he'd mortgage his best song to a white blues guitar god? guess he did, but even if exile on main street looking back has some amazing songs on it was it any more or less amazing as records by other bands that year? seventy-two gave us let's stay together by al green and neil's harvest and pink moon by nick drake and aretha's young gifted and black and something/anything by todd and, shit, pink floyd debuted dark side of the moon in january and ry cooder released into the purple valley and deep purple did machine head and big star had a number one record and randy newman came out with sail away and little feat — little feat! — had sailin' shoes and june gave us ziggy stardust roxy music lou reed and school's out by the coop and the harder they come and t rex's the slider and son of schmilsson and the band's rock of ages and backstabbers and all the young dudes by mott and even close to the edge by yes and a month later there was heavy cream and clear spot by captain beefheart and can't buy a thrill and another al green album called i'm still in love with you and in november neil followed up harvest with journey through the past and marlo thomas put out a kid's record that everyone owned called free to be . . . you and me and the year ended with trouble man by marvin gaye and lou reed's transformer because back then he shat songs faster than anyone could record them. so here were the stones — surviving detroit despite cops carrying axe-handled clubs and aerosol cans and pistols and then surging towards the border — and while their tour was the biggest and most unruly in rock and roll history it was crowded at the top man: shit they weren't even the biggest deal that weekend in a protestant backwater like toronto, ontario, i mean can you believe it?

On Thursday, NDP leader David Lewis asked External Affairs Minister Mitchell Sharp "whether the government has been officially or in any other way informed by the government of France regarding the alleged ramming of *Greenpeace III* by a French minesweeper." Sharp responded by telling him that, "I asked our embassy in France to get in touch with the French government because we had no information previously about the incident . . . there are conflicting reports about the collision. The French . . . said essentially that the two ships were passing slowly alongside each other, the French ship about to pass a message to the *Greenpeace*. The *Greenpeace* turned by mistake, or was blown into the French ship. Damage was light, but the *Greenpeace* asked for help and was towed to Mururoa and repaired free of charge. The crew was hospitably treated."

Hairy-armed and muscle-jawed, Bobby Hull was like the quarter-pounder of hockey. He was the ABC Movie of the Week, the alkaline flats' landspeed supercar, Secretariat, Mario Puzo, Brando, *Who's Next*, Jean-Claude Killy, Erich Segal's *Love Story,* Ronco's Veg-O-Matic and Patty Stacker, John Lennon on *Mike Douglas,* Marvel and DC, *The Computer Who Wore Tennis Shoes,* Richard Harris's "MacArthur Park," platform shoes and denim caps, "Keep on Truckin'," Rod Laver in white shorts, Chianti wine in wicker-covered globes, flower-patched bell-bottom jeans worn with a burlap belt, Elton John's sunglasses, Philly Soul, Jimmy Page's doubleneck and John Bonham's gong, mood rings, trucking songs, the films of George Romero, Freddie Mercury's crotch pack, Stevie Wonder on *Sesame Street,* Let it be Dicey or Let it be Nothing, Ali vs. Frazier, Lolas, velvet bullfighter paintings, *Jonathan Livingston Seagull, Battle of the Network Stars,* songs about what it was like to be a native Indian by performers who weren't native Indians, jai alai, Sid and Marty Krofft, Happiness is . . . , sad Cat Stevens music, the Sweathogs, *Trilogy of Terror,* "Seven Words You Can Never Say on Television," aerosol, unisex, "Disco Duck," jumpsuit chest hair, Hertz vs. Avis, *The Courtship of Eddie's Father,* "Jive Talkin'," OPEC, Lance Kerwin, Hot Wheels, Sanka, Bottle Caps, Quisp, Dynamints, Lik-A-Stix, "Sit on it!," dime bags and tube tops, PCP, ELP, and GRT, strip malls and smoke and gifts, the death of The Beatles, Morton Shulman, Don Kirshner, Blaxsploitation, sniffing PAM, Love's Baby Soft shampoo, Creepy Crawlers, "Wango Tango," *Going Down the Road,* Rick Azar and Commander Tom and Ed Shaunessy on the drums, Ancient Chinese Secret, Jesus as a groovy kind of dude, Molson Extra Old Stock, Gee Your Hair Smells Terrific!, a Longines Symphonette, Hoyt Axton eight-tracks, lip gloss, roto-toms and flashpots and the music known as southern boogie, "decent" and "cool" and "gross me out" and "hey, man, flood's over," Richard Nixon masks on Halloween, white skates, lavish pubic hair, Thai stick, Italian–American film-makers in Hollywood, douching commercials, 7 Burps, Dr. Pepper, "Adriaaaaannnnn!!!", Fruit of the Loom, *Chariot of the Gods,* Norman MacLaren's *Neighbours,* Steve Martin's Wild and Crazy Guy, the Laurie Bower Singers, Sometimes You Feel Like a Nut, Sometimes You Don't, the AFL, ABA, and, right there, in the pulp of his middle-aged life, Bobby Hull's fledg-ling new hockey league – the WHA – which would eventually feature teams called the Los Angeles Sharks, Baltimore Blades, Denver Spurs, Ottawa Nationals, Toronto Toros, New York Blades, and Vancouver Blazers. Hull was all of these things, but on Thursday, he discovered one thing that he was not. The goddamned NHL owners had gotten their way.

He was not a member of Team Canada.

On Thursday, Jim Slotek gathered all of the stuff that he needed to fly to Toronto, which, because he was a teenager, wasn't much. His parents were nervous – planes were being hijacked every day – but he really wanted to go, and besides, his brother was going to be there, so he'd have someone to show him around. He was fourteen and in love with rock and roll. Toronto had poster shops, record stores, clubs, and cafes. It had Yonge Street, where Master John's sold platform shoes with little aquariums and fish swimming around in the heels, and Flashjacks sold pipes and bongs and chillums and vials of methyl nitrate and Big Bambu rolling papers, to say nothing of racks of Farrah Fawcett and Rolling Stones and Jimi Hendrix and *Dirty Harry* posters, and the occasional brown paper bag that concealed smuggled VHS and BETA copies of *Behind the Green Door, Debbie Does Dallas,* or *Insatiable,* the horny teen-ager's holy trinity of seventies porn. There were also all of those strip bars (the Brass Rail, Zanzibars), clubs (the Picadilly Circus, the Gasworks), as well as porno theatres, like Cinema 2000. The strip was seedy and wild and tough, as far from a prairie town as anyone in the 1970s could imagine.

Jim's visit to Mariposa '72 was his first time in Toronto. He remembers: "I went with my brother, who was ten years older. It wasn't the sixties, but there were elements of hippie culture and all of that, being pre-disco, which would happen shortly thereafter. Walking around looking at everyone at the festival, it felt, to me, like the whole scene had fallen out of the sky. At one point, some lady started running around, shouting, 'Joe Cocker's here! Joe Cocker's here!' And it caused a commotion, for whatever reason. I remember seeing Lightfoot play. This was a big deal, at least to me; I knew all of his songs on guitar; most people did at the time. At one point, he sat down on a rock and started playing. A small crowd gathered around him."

Jim came to Toronto at a time when scenes and movements and sounds were both dying and being born. Nineteen seventy-two was both the beginning and the end of a distinct era in Canadian music and culture. It was the end of Yorkville's songwriters scene and the beginning of Yonge Street's rock band era. It was the end of colonial media and the beginning of Canada-centric TV programs – *The Trouble with Tracy, The King of Kensington* and *The Beachcombers,* which debuted in September, 1972 – as well as two new important networks: Global television and Citytv, both of which were launched in 1972, and whose stock-in-trade was raw, shocking television (in the U.S.A., HBO launched that same summer). One evening, Global showed the country a drunken, damaged, and forlorn Derek Sanderson interviewed by Mike Anscombe, with a drink in one hand and a cigarette in the other. Moses Znaimer's Citytv, broadcasting from a brownstone in downtown Toronto, went even further, broadcasting local chat shows where kids smoked pot and feather-masked swingers espoused the freedoms of sexual adventure. Nineteen seventy-two was also the end of public radio as a tweedy, classically driven BBC sound-alike and the beginning of Terry David Mulligan's *90 Minutes with a Bullet.* It was the end of a country defined only by the power of the land and the beginning of an urban renaissance. It was the end of Newfoundland's premier, Joey Smallwood, and the beginning of any local politician other than him. It was the end of Canada feeling inferior for being large and young and beautiful and the beginning of a time when, as we moved our hands from our eyes, we found that being large and young and beautiful wasn't such a bad thing. It was the end of Bobby Gimby and the beginning of "American Woman." It was the end of "From New York to L.A." and the beginning of "My Stompin' Grounds." It was the end of "One Fine Morning" and the beginning of "Taking Care of Business." In 1972, Canada seemed to find its volume knob. Even if it didn't know exactly what it was saying, it was saying it louder than ever.

The changes in Canada – and, specifically, Toronto – were triggered by outside influences as much as they were self-started. Singer/actor/writer Gale Zoe Garnett who, by 1972, had already gone through several lives as a pop star, said that Toronto's kinship with New York directly affected local culture, going so far as to point to a single event that, she said, helped move one city closer to the other, and one decade out of the next. "From my perspective, everything changed after Bette Midler played the Continental Baths in New York City," she told me. "Afterwards, art and society and popular culture became very different from what they'd been before. At the Baths, there was always red liquid in the water cooler. Guys were running around with their towels tied on different sides to signify what they were or weren't into, and I grabbed one of them and pointed to the red liquid and I asked: 'Campari?' He replied: 'No, Lavoris [a mouthwash].' It was one of my favourite moments."

By crossing into the burgeoning gay culture of the early 1970s New York, Midler, says Garnett, introduced the hetero-sexual world to the homosexual world, sending music and art down a new, unexplored path. "Because there was such a huge exchange between New York and Toronto, you could see the effect that it had in Canada. People would go down there, experience new things, and bring them north, and in this came the ultimate end of the 1960s. The sixties era was very het. It wasn't homophobic, but its physical look and its design was very het, and so was the musical culture, whether it was acoustic or electric. The whole disco thing – which originally came from France – became gayified, and it opened things up. There was a place called Reno Sweeneys in New York. I played there once, opening for the singer Peter Allen. I did some songs and a few funny or dramatic scenes. After my set, someone came backstage to tell me that theatre critic and translator Eric Bentley and Julie Christie were in the audience and she wanted to meet me. When I went out to see them at their table, Lou Reed was sitting there as well. I told him how much I loved his music and that I was a big fan. He looked me over and asked me, 'Oh yeah? Do you want to suck my cock?' I said the first time thing came into my head: 'I dunno? Does it sing?'"

Garnett is insistent that end of the sixties and the beginning of seventies was marked by the change in recreational drug use: the rainbow mellow of pot giving way to coke's harder edge. "It started in 1969 with the Hell's Angels at Altamont. I'd heard that they were doing coke as well as selling it. Coke didn't get big until around '72, and it changed – I don't know – the tenor of things. The thing with coke is that it's such a power trip. The immortality kicks in just as the power kicks in. I didn't do a lot of coke – it's hard to do

Shakespeare with your nose running – but, one time, I was driving down Bloor Street in Toronto and I heard myself say, 'That's one really ugly building. They should blow that fucker up.' I stopped in that interstitial place between feeling wonderful and realizing that I was becoming a power-tripping asshole with nose and tooth problems. If the sixties were about the pervading mellow that pot provided, then coke came along and smashed it to bits with an enormous hammer. The whole aura of the times was suddenly very, very different."

The first album I ever bought was in the summer of 1972. While I don't know the exact date of the album's release – nor does the Internet, apparently – my narrative impulses want it to be deep summer, say the second week of July, and just as the stars are showing up on the island or the Stones are climbing the stage at Maple Leaf Gardens or Pioneer 10 is tickling the asteroid belt, I'm shelling out three dollars and ninety-nine cents of my folks' money before carrying the record under my arm to the family car where I stare from the back seat at the weird names of great and not-great bands whose songs I would know front to back before the end of the weekend. The album pushed me into a world of joy until, decades later, I ended up writing songs of my own in a band of my own. In the summer of 1972, I had no idea this would ever happen, even though it's what I wanted more than anything.

The album was *Believe in Music*, K-Tel's sun-splashed compilation. Its cover had orange, red, and pink streaks of light

— happy-pop colours — radiating from the top right corner of the jacket over the photo of a festival crowd, with broad seventies script announcing the record's name as well as "22 Original Hits/Original Stars." The album started with "Brandy" by Looking Glass — a group from New Jersey, who, two years later, would change their name twice, from Fallen Angels to Starz, before splitting for good — and ended with Gallery's "I Believe in Music," the compilation record's eponymous title cut. Sandwiched in between were songs by The Raspberries ("Go All the Way"), Donny Osmond ("Go Away Little Girl"), Dr. Hook ("Sylvia's Mother"), and Argent ("Hold Your Head Up") among others. The first time I peeled off the shrink wrap and played it on the pale wood-grained eight-track, turntable, cassette deck, and radio monolith in our pale wood-grained basement, I listened to both sides with my parents sitting across from me on the couch. I remember how excited they were that I was excited, and how, in the end, the album wasn't a truncheon or a knife that divided us. Instead, we listened to songs like "Let Your Yeah Be Yeah" by Brownsville Station and nodded along together, although The Raspberries' teenage sex ballad made me feel a little weird. Still, for these reasons, rock and roll has always been less about outright rebellion for me, and more about a way of getting along.

Small record stores are rare today, but they were everywhere in the new suburban landscape of my youth. I shopped for records at places like Music World at the Albion Mall, A&A's at Sherway Gardens, Sam the Record Man at Royal York Plaza, and Sunrise Records at Cloverdale Mall. Half of these stores were in strip malls, wedged between bowling alleys and Laura Secord chocolate shops. Before I started buying music myself, I'd watch as older kids stood at the counter pointing to one of the singles – arranged forty to one in order of chart position on a wall – which the clerk grabbed and slid A-side up across the countertop. Once I got older, I'd hear a great song on my bicycle's handlebar radio – "Frankenstein" by Edgar Winter Group, "Mull of Kintyre" by Wings, or anything by The Sweet – then go after school to buy it. Clive Davis could have built a mansion with my Christmas money.

In the seventies, music wasn't only sold in proper record stores. Sal's IGA had an album rack that stood where *US* and *People* magazines are sold today. All of the hardware stores sold albums, too, and so did Becker's Milk, a variety store serviced by label jobbers and independent distributers. I'd go to the plaza with my mom, and while she made the rounds – drugstore, shoe repair, bakery, dry cleaner, supermarket – I'd hang out in the Becker's, draining a box of chocolate milk while turning the new Alice Cooper or Flying Burrito Brothers album over in my hands. The first time I ever heard of musicians like Laura Nyro or the Pure Prairie League was at that store. By the time we got home I'd have already torn off the shrink wrap and would wing the vinyl onto the turntable that my parents had allowed me to move into my room.

Besides the local strip mall depots, there were two Toronto record stores that every kid in the seventies knew about, and tried to go to at least once a week: Sam the Record Man and A&A's on Yonge Street. For me, it was like going to Maple Leaf

Gardens or the CN Tower or City Hall. They were temples of vinyl with a great cardboard fresco of album faces patterned across the walls. Both stores had three floors with new and old releases spilling out of the racks. It might be hard for a modern kid raised on downloads and the private absorption of music to imagine the scene – seventies record stores are to twenty-first-century kids what malt shops were to me – but the scene on Saturday afternoon at Sam's downtown collected everyone who loved music in the city buying and listening and consuming together. Their Boxing Day sale – which offered half-price vinyl and British import bargains – made the national news, and David Bowie autograph signings caused riots. Before concerts at the Gardens, only two blocks away, people didn't go for dinner or drinks before the shows – they went to Sam's. The store drew kids from every corner of the city – and province – and, in my early days playing music, I met musicians hanging out there, struck up friendships, formed a rock and roll bond. The store closed a few years ago, as have most record shops. Like a lot of what's in this book, all that's left are the stories.

In 1979, I got a chance to work in a record store. It was something I'd always wanted to do. I was sixteen years old and summering as an employee at Music World in the Albion Mall, a job that my father – a shopping mall builder – helped me land. At first, the job was fine, almost dream-like. I got to hang McCartney *Back to the Egg* posters on the wall, hook "California Jam" T-shirts on the swag rack and test promo records that publicists sent to us every Tuesday; albums by Emigre, Flash in the Pan, and The Monks. Since punk rock hadn't really hit Etobicoke, the closest we came to mirroring the record shop in Nick Hornby's *High Fidelity* was daring to play *Bop till You Drop* by Ry Cooder, Carolyne Mas, *Damn the Torpedoes,* or, if there was no one looking, *Look Sharp* by Joe Jackson. My boss, a woman named Frances, played Dylan's *At Budokan* every morning (she also played it after lunch and twice in the evening, too). I couldn't understand Dylan back then, partly because Cheap Trick had also released a record called *Live at Budokan,* which I loved. It bothered me that someone who was considered a genius couldn't have come up with another, more original, name for his album. One afternoon, I told Frances that we should play the two records back to back, wanting to prove how much better I thought Cheap Trick's record was. Frances shook her head, lit another du Maurier and told me that, um, well, no, we wouldn't be doing that. Then she told me to take down the J. Geils Band poster and put up a poster for Billy Joel's *Glass Houses,* which I thought was a kind of harsh punishment.

Apart from the fact that I knew every song from every album and every musician who played in every band that year, I was terrible at my job. I'd leave the cash register open and walk away, give incorrect change, wander for hours in the mall past lunchtime, hang posters that fell down, and break stuff I hadn't meant to break. I also grabbed promo records for myself, and posters, too: Dwight Twilley, The Fabulous Poodles, Steely Dan. Frances said that we were supposed to send them back to the record companies, but that seemed ridiculous. I wanted to steal the *Back to the Egg* poster, too, but it was too big.

Things got worse for me after they hired a person to work evenings, and to watch over me during my afternoon shifts. She was a fiftysomething Scottish woman who hated music, and hated me more. Her actual job was to make sure I didn't give away too much change or allow shoplifters to shoplift too easily, but her unofficial job was to make sure that I got fired so that her nephew could work there. She smoked menthol Benson & Hedges and never smiled. She took people's money, bagged the albums, and played *At Budokan* over and over, because she thought it's what the boss wanted. One afternoon, Frances told her that she might be playing it a little bit too much. I said that we'd been sent the new record by Graham Parker and the Rumour and had heard it was good. She told the old woman to play it, so she did. From "Discovering Japan" to "Passion Ain't No Ordinary Word," she smoked and looked balefully at me.

Having to deal with my sour workmate didn't help, but, in the end, I blew the gig on my own. I was fired just before the summer ended. They told me that I didn't have what it took, and that the old lady's nephew would be taking over my job. I asked if I could have the Joe Jackson poster that hung in the office. Frances said that I could. I went back there and folded *Back to the Egg* into the *Look Sharp* poster, and put them on my wall in our basement in Etobicoke, where, each time I looked at them, I was reminded that the world of selling stuff was no world for me. Soon it would be 1980, and, in October, the Rheostatics did their first gig. The seventies were over.

LETTER IN WHICH I CALL YOU A SELL-OUT (EVEN THOUGH YOU ARE NOT)

So Gord, you gave in. You sold out. You fell prey to what you vowed you'd never be. I'm kidding, actually. I'm kidding, but it's true that what you did in 1957 was something no one ever thought you'd do: you wrote a rock and roll song, or at least a novelty rock and roll song, about Hula Hoops. The musical experts out here wonder whether the idea of becoming famous and popular and making a living led you to this choice. One dude, quoted anonymously in Collins' book, said, "If disco was popular back then, he would have done that, too." Whatever the impulse, it's hard to explain the embrace of a form you'd steered away from without drawing that conclusion. Then again, maybe you just really liked Hula Hoops. They are fun. I've got to admit that.

Collins says that it's the first song you ever wrote, but I find that hard to believe (still, remember, you won't talk to me, so I don't know for sure). Anyway, you borrowed your dad's car and you headed back to Toronto, where you met Harold Moon, a publisher at BMI. Moon was a good guy, and he treated you with respect, even though you were only seventeen. I imagine that drive into town being the kind that most hopeful and budding artists take, believing that on the other end of the journey lies the great first payoff, the initial validation, the moment when you suddenly break through the thing that you've been butting against for most of your life. In the end, Moon didn't want the song, but it was okay. He looked at you across his big publishing-executive desk filled with papers and pens and stacks of sheet music and certificates framed on the wall behind him and he told you something that was almost as good as a publishing deal. He told you not to give up.

So you didn't. Instead, in 1958, you decided to go to Los Angeles, to the Westlake School of Modern Music. You liked jazz and had started playing drums with the Charlie Andrews Orchestra in Orillia. You read *Downbeat* – no, you devoured *Downbeat* – you and your pal Buddy Hill. At Westlake, you studied piano, orchestration, and musical theory. Lenny Soloman, the fiddler and violinist, told me: "Gordon has a real musicality. I did a session with him in 1974 or '75, and I got called to play some fiddle. It was a real eye-opener because he was so musically intelligent, not in the way I expected from a folksinger. He knew the chords, the flat five, all of the time signatures. He didn't need someone to translate his ideas for him. He was a musician first, and anyone not involved with him at that level couldn't have appreciated his knowledge."

Another story, from comic Harry Doupe, who met you at the Junos in 1996: "I was writing for the show. Aside from the Hall of Fame inductees, the only nod to the past was Gord singing 'If You Could Read My Mind.' I was at rehearsal at Copps Coliseum in Hamilton, and I was sitting at the front. They started up the tune, Gord began singing and he was horrible. His voice was just ridiculously bad. They ran through the song; reset, did it a few more times. It got slightly better, but we were like, 'Man, this is the last time he'll be on the show.' He did it more and more and it got a little better each time. He did it seven times. Then, he wanted a break. Anne Murray was supposed to host, and she needed to run through her bit, so organizers were nervous about running out of rehearsal time. Gord was in his room for half an hour at least. When he finally came out, he did it one more time and it was amazing. After the song finished, he said, 'I saved the best one for last because Annie's here.'"

Doug McClement remembers working with you in Reno, Nevada, in the nineties. He was recording sound for a TV special using his mobile-studio truck. He told me: "Lightfoot has a system that has worked for decades, and he's neurotic about changing anything. When we did the show in Reno, the set designers asked if they could change the carpet that is used on stage under the band. Gord said no. When the keyboard player asked if he could move a keyboard onto a different stand to make it easier to play one of the songs, Gord said no. When the sound department wanted to swap out the mic on the acoustic guitar for a smaller one, Gord said no. They ended up doing a two-hour soundcheck, essentially playing the entire show end to end. These guys had been playing the same songs for sixteen years, probably hundreds of times over. After soundcheck, Gordon came into the mobile, sat at the console, closed his eyes, and listened to the entire recording. He made notes, then went back to the band with some changes. He wasn't being a jerk. He was just very meticulous and very much in control of his entire presentation. When Bob Doidge did the final mix at Grant Avenue Studios in Hamilton, Gordon came in, spent a lot of time setting the volume levels on each track, then instructed Bob not to touch anything during the mix. So, like a good jazz group, the dynamics were all controlled by the musicians themselves. No fader moves."

Okay: Los Angeles. Back then, it was as weird as it's always been. It was probably weirder for you, when you consider that you'd never lived anywhere other than Orillia. You left L.A. after two years. It happens. A lot of my friends have gone to L.A., too. And New York; Canadians looking for something greater to the south. It's hard to resist reaching out and trying to get whatever you can, because a little bit of America can go a long way.

You probably never met her, Gord — you were hanging out mostly with music students — but did you ever hear of the songwriter Sharon Sheeley? My friend, Ken Tobias, met her when he moved to California in the sixties to write for Bert Sugarman's publishing house. I know this is a book about you, Gord, but I hope you won't mind me telling a story about Ken. You might even like it. It's a California story by way of Canada, if that makes a difference at all.

Ken met Sharon while meditating by a small fountain at an old Hollywood monastery that had been converted into an apartment/loft house. Ken might hate me for saying this, but I'm pretty sure that he had a suave, Greek Island Jesus–beard at the time, and wore bell-bottoms with hippie bracelets and probably had a mood stone hanging around his neck. Sharon, on the other hand, was dressed elegantly, if casually. She was a slender beauty with long black hair. She wasn't young – she was maybe fifty at the time – but in the fifties, she had been a member of Elvis's entourage ("She only had good things to say about him," said Ken). She asked Ken what he did for a living and Ken told her that he was a songwriter from Canada signed to Bill Medley's company. Sharon said that she was a songwriter, too. She invited Ken to have a cold drink and later told him that she had written "Poor Little Fool" for Ricky Nelson and "Dum Dum" for Brenda Lee. I know that you didn't go to California to be a songwriter, Gord – that happened later, and it didn't even happen because you were hustling your songs; it just happened because you were good and people liked them; people like Elvis – but back then, in Ken's day, the roads were lousy with songwriters trying to get their stuff bought and sold. When Ken first went to Bert Sugarman's office, he ran into Mac Davis, who told him that he thought maybe, just maybe, Elvis was going to do one of his tunes, either "Memories" or "In the Ghetto" or both. Anyhow, Ken didn't really have a lot of luck, but he did meet Sharon Sheeley. And, in a way, that was maybe even luckier or better than selling a song to Elvis.

Sharon told Ken that, after she wrote "Poor Little Fool," she walked past Ricky Nelson's beach house every day until she finally met him. She played the song for him and he loved it. When Sharon was a teenager, she hung around with Gene Vincent and Eddie Cochran, whom she started dating. She was a blue jeans model, but she also wrote songs, although, because she was a woman, no one in the music business took her seriously, which is weird because people like Ellie Greenwich and Carole King had made lots of people loads of money, although they weren't blue jeans models and they weren't as sexy or as beautiful as Sharon. After she wrote "Sweet Nothings," they credited the song to her brother, and co-credited Eddie Cochran with the composition, even though Sharon had written it. It made it to the Top Ten, but Sharon didn't garner much respect. She ended up going to England with Gene and Eddie, and things turned out pretty badly for all of them.

One night after a show, they decided to drive to the next gig. The driver was young and cocky and he drove fast, trying to impress his heroes. He lost control of the car, and when police sorted through the wreckage, Eddie Cochran was found dead with his arm over his guitar case. Sharon and Gene ended up in the hospital. Fans sent Sharon flowers, and telegrams poured in from around the world. She showed Ken old *Photoplay* magazines with pictures of her in her hospital bed.

Ken was never romantically involved with Sharon, but he was deeply fond of her. She helped him get through California, through Los Angeles, while suffering the anxiety of a musician trying to make it in the U.S.A. Sharon knew everyone in the music scene. After awhile, she gained the respect she deserved, and won citations for her songwriting. Sharon introduced Ken to his heroes: Don and Phil Everly. One evening, Don arrived in a vintage Cadillac to pick him up, but when Ken got in the back seat, he was shaking. Sharon grabbed him and whispered, "Do not approach these guys as a fan. They think of you as a fellow musician, so straighten up." Eventually, Ken returned to Canada and lost touch with Sharon. I don't know if you consider yourself lucky, Gord, and I'm not suggesting that you are. All I'm saying is that sometimes people don't get the break they deserve, and sometimes people die without anyone ever knowing how good they were. But I'm probably telling you something you already know and feel a little foolish for having said it.

So: L.A. City in the smog is what Neil Young called it. I wonder whether those thoughts that you had that night on the dock of the Big Chief – or maybe you didn't have them; remember: I'm imagining – but I wonder whether they came more clearly into focus while you were there. Tom Waits, and others, have said, "Sometimes it takes being thousands of miles away before you ever really know your home," and I'd like to think that, the smell of the pine and the sap and the fireplace smoke became stronger, more profound, the farther you were away from it. I think of you smelling the snow – I wonder if you can even smell snow; I think you can – or the wet, oily scent of the fish greased in your hands after you and your dad had pulled it from lake or the cedar insides of the cabin or the bacon frying in the cast-iron pan that your grandparents used, and their grandparents before that. Maybe you could hear the sounds, too, the ones that filled your ears as a boy; resonant and strong despite being muffled by the torrent of life in an American city. I wonder whether, from these things, you drew a certain artistic strength. Maybe, after finding this strength, you thought to yourself, "Man, how am I supposed to express this through jazz?" even though, when you listen to Louis Armstrong, you can hear the city of New Orleans, or, when you listen to Roland Kirk, the sounds of the Pacific crawling through his flutes and whatever other crazy woodwinds and horns he liked to play. Still, if it wasn't jazz, it would be something else, and, looking back, it's crazy how obvious it seems in retrospect. After all, this music had been around forever. It just had to be reborn.

Folk music.

You moved to Toronto. You didn't feel defeated. No, you felt strong. Yorkville was coming, and when it came: man. Still, you worked as a bank teller at Yonge and Eglinton – your dad got you the job through his connections – and you met a woman, Brita, a beautiful Swedish girl, whom you married. You went to Stockholm for the wedding, and took your honeymoon in Lillehammer, the village where they staged the Olympics a few decades later, and where Canada won silver in hockey, although they would have won gold, if only Paul Kariya had buried his shot top-corner instead of drilling it into Tommy Salo's pads. There was domestic life – you had a son, Fred – but there was music, too. You got a gig on a corny CBC program, *Country Hoedown,* but, Christ, it was work. Good work, too. They called you "Gordon Leadfoot," but, heck, you were on national TV, dancing and singing in a chorus and doing the two-step. You started playing. More and more and more. You met Ian Tyson and he showed you some chords. You stayed up all night learning old songs, and some new ones, too. Then an offer came through to host your own TV program in Britain, at which point everything went cloudy. You were far away, and only Brita, and your mom, who came to help out, know what it was like. But let me take a stab at it. I went to Britain, too. With the band. To London, England. We fought and lost our drummer. Did it turn out better or worse for you?

You went there on a plane. 1963. Back then, flying was an event. When I think of flying in the 1960s, I think of all of those old colour-drenched movies that show airports as great palaces of comfort and progress, and how people would dress up just to meet friends coming home from places like Crete or Thailand or Windsor Castle or Palm Springs. The buildings looked like Walt Disney's idea of the future: signs emblazoned with the cool blue and red and orange airline logos of the day – TWA, CP Air, Pan Am – clicking and blinking on big boards as you entered the building. I think of bun-haired stewardesses with smart little hats tipped to one side and painted lips and long fingernails carrying martini trays and dark chocolates in paper cups, selling cigarettes, too, if you wanted them, which back then, everyone did. And then I think of how you might have felt coming in as a kid with country roots – almost every-one was a business traveller back then, or else wealthy enough to afford the ticket price – and how maybe, while in transit over some enormous body of water glistening in the sun, you thought that the other men and women flying could smell the shit on the heels of your boots. Or maybe you blunted the feeling, thinking that you were where you were supposed to be – rubbing elbows with Stan the rubber-band magnate – and the dazzle was normal because you were going to England, to London. And you were going to be a star.

There are no tapes of the show, so no one really knows how you did. You were the host: "And now ladies and gentlemen, all the way from the Isle of Wight . . ." Maybe you realized pretty fast that this wasn't your ticket, and maybe the producers realized this, too, because the show bottomed out. But still, it was 1963. It was the greatest time for pop music ever. The Beatles, The Stones, The Kinks, and The Who. I think that says it all right there. Did you ever see any of them? Did you run into Mick or Keith in the hallways, or did you turn away whenever they came past, grumbling to yourself for being this hayseed marquee wannabe when the very consciousness of young men and women around the western world was being played out in the music around you? Or did you think they were just a bunch of stupid poseurs, because that's what a lot of them were, despite the genius songs and heavy, heavy albums. Me, I would have felt burned. I would have turned the corner outside the studio and seen parades of kids in Carnaby Street whistling Small Faces songs wondering whether I'd tried too hard instead of letting whatever it is I'd wanted to become find me naturally. Or maybe I would have pounced into the fray trying to grab whatever I could from the rock and roll mania of the day. But you didn't do that. When you came back to Canada, there was as little influence of British pop and rock on your music as there had been when American music exploded in the late fifties. Maybe, instead, you just quietly stewed in your Chelsea flat. You smelled the cedar and told yourself to just get the fuck back to Canada.

Yorkville. There's nothing left – well, okay, the Pilot Tavern is left, and there's a little plaque where the Riverboat used to be – but if you listen closely, if you sit at the picnic table in the field of the Jesse Ketchum school and close your eyes, you can almost dream it alive. I'm not being romantic – or at least I'm trying not to – but it would have been pretty fun to be there. The sex was easy, the gigs plentiful, the boarding houses cheap and clean. The singers were good, the guitar players accomplished, and every night you watched them and told yourself that you'd be better, leaving them gasping over their own inadequacies. Okay, maybe not that chick Joni, with her otherworldly face and voice that climbed like a small animal up a tree. And maybe not that Neil dude, either, who grinned and smoke doped and hid behind his band until somebody passed him a guitar, which he fingered awkwardly, all thumbs and twisted fingers, making weird chords to songs about spacemen and hawks and winter that produced a strange beauty despite the obvious clumsiness and endearing ugly of the man. Maybe not David Whiffen, either, and maybe not the kid Cockburn. And probably not Ian and Sylvia, Sylvia being the hottest piece of ass on the Cumberland strip, and Ian her handsome and manly equal. But for every one of them, there were countless manger mouths and pretenders in caftans and shawls and fringed jackets. But you'd show them the soil, drown them in the lake. You'd feed them snow and the country until they were genuflecting at your boots.

Along with the musicians, there were the hangers-on, but more than that, there were the mooks who came from elsewhere. Since Yorkville was the Toronto hub of free love, they arrived from every corner of the city and its broad new suburbs, their ideas gleaned from sensational *Weekend Magazine* photo essays. They didn't care about the music so much as the promise of fast girls with rainbow-painted titties. They came wanting to fake their way into an orgy, but, most times, they got drunk on Triple X and settled for a fight. Want to know why the sixties failed? Ask them. They wanted a wild ride without any of the bends or stomach pain that came with hard work. It was a responsibility which, as an artist, you were forced to assume.

It was a good party, yeah, but even then, you went sideways. You did your own thing, finding a joint on Yonge Street, Steele's Tavern, which was run by Pop Steeles, who booked you thirty times in one year. It was your kind of place: hard-drinking and boisterous and alive. The hippies hardly ever came down. Instead, there were students and working stiffs. You knew that if you could hush these people with your songs, you could work anywhere. The gigs were hell on your marriage. You were out late. This one threw herself at you. That one had a nice little place around the corner. Climbing on stage, people saw this figure — tall, denimed, with sharp features and a serious voice – and even though they cried for you to play standards, you gave them your own stuff every now and then, songs like "For Lovin' You," your first great song. You were handsome and you were cool, in an unaffected and totemic northern way. It's what almost every guy I interviewed said: how striking you were. One of them even told me, "Listen, I'm married and everything, but Gord was just, you know, beautiful." The buzz started to set in and you could see a rich and fulfilling musical life ahead of you the way one sees the lights of a town after driving by themselves down a long empty road in the middle of the night on less than a quarter of a tank of gas.

One evening, Ian and Sylvia came to see you. A ripple of excitement came over the dark, wood-panelled tavern because they'd already had hit records, but instead of drawing attention to themselves, they stood cross-armed and out of the light at the back of the room. Afterwards, Tyson said that he would get Albert Grossman's man, John Court, to check out the show. He did. Court liked it. You were good, or at least you were getting good. Court said that he wanted you to sign with them. Dylan's manager. Bob Dylan. Then he said those words that you'd been waiting to hear most of your life: "Gordon, we want you to come to New York City."

'72

FRIDAY, JULY 14TH

On Friday morning, the Mariposa Folk Festival opened. Thousands gathered on the cement dock of the mainland's ferry terminal before passing through its tall white gates and along a narrow metal ramp to the boats. It was an old sound: feet stamping on the great wooden deck as a storm of voices rang throughout the vessel. People crammed buoy to buoy as the foghorn bellowed and the ferry started to move, engines growling as the hull knocked against the waves, spraying those who stood along the railing. The skies were grey and it was raining – lightly at first, then a little heavier as the day wore on – but it didn't matter. Careering into the island dock, the ship lowered its gangway and the festival-goers exited bandanaed and sandaled, their pipes stuffed in rucksacks, dope hidden in socks, granola bagged, and fruit and beer and other things chilled in Coleman coolers. Younger kids (seventies kids, although they wouldn't have called themselves that at the time) wearing Mott the Hoople top hats and striped pants wandered towards the festival site along the shore of the island's dark canals, while another, smaller group – drugged, wild-haired, and dizzy-eyed – ran from the dock in search of the strongest crook in the longest branch of the tallest tree, from which they would observe the whole of the festival, occasionally mewling and scratching at the wind.

People were handed newsprint programs from volunteers standing inside the red snow-fence that separated the event from the rest of the island. The program's cover had an aboriginal image of a loon painted by Saul Williams, an eighteen-year-old Ojibway kid from Weagamow, Ontario, whose work would be collected and shown, two decades later, at the Royal Ontario Museum. The back cover featured an illustration by

Mariposa on Centre Island, 1972

Adrienne Leban: a full-colour, pointillist rendering of planets revolving around the sun with a celestialography of half moons, arrows, and sixty-nines drawn at the top of the page. The date and time was scribbled in freehand at the bottom: 14 July, 10:30 a.m., Toronto, Canada. The rest of the program was filled with odd bits – an ad for Yorkdale Shopping Centre ("Canada's Fashion Centre"), TSS recording studio, BMI music, a local Gulf service station, the Brau Haus restaurant, and Stompin' Tom's label, Boot Records – but none was odder than a favourable two-page auditor's report from the 1971 festival published on pages twenty-five and twenty-six. There were also extensive artist bios and photos teeming with shawled women and sideburned men as well as a strange essay called "Videovision versus Television."

The crowd – which, by Saturday morning, would grow to be 14,000 strong – settled in front of the six stages, people laying out their blankets on the damp summer grass. There were guitars – lots of guitars – and mandolins, too. Colin Puffer, who was studying at York University at the time, re-members: "I brought my guitar to Mariposa not necessarily intending to play with anyone, but to participate in work-shops. These days, workshops feature musicians who play their three most popular songs, hoping to sell CDs in the merchandise tent. But back then, workshops were exactly what that word suggested." Puffer recalls: "That was the thing about Mariposa back then. You'd leave the festival having learned so much about music. You'd improve as a musician by watching and, in this case, by doing."

Musician Ken Whiteley played his first Mariposa in 1972, as a member of the Original Sloth Band. "I've always said that I didn't go to university," he tells me, "I went to folk festivals. There was so much to learn and to absorb. In '72, I sat around playing with David Wilcox and Peter Ecklund, the trumpet player [Gregg Allman, Paul Butterfield], and we had this swing jam. Ted Bogan joined in and he taught me swing chords I never knew before. At a later festival, I remember playing with Dewey Balfa and listening to him say, 'Now, there are six different ways to accompany a Cajun waltz.' By the end of every Mariposa, I'd absorbed so much."

Gordon Klager, the Ottawa hostel kid and Crowbar fan, hitchhiked to the festival because, he said, "Mariposa '72 was one of the first gatherings of the tribes. Before '72, hippie culture was only in Toronto, but it had started to spread, and one of the things about that weekend was that everyone was coming together. You watch the movie, *Festival Express,* which was made in 1970, and pretty much everyone in the crowd has short hair. But the freaks were out in '72, and you could feel that on the island. The festival had the feeling of triumph for our culture. It was as if, after years of fighting against trad-itional ways and values and all of that, people just said, 'Fuck it,' and did whatever they wanted. I battled with my father about my beard and my hair and other things, but by 1972, I'd just worn him down. They got tired of fighting us."

With consecutive boatloads, the grounds eventually became packed with people like Klager, festival-goers crack-ing beers, pouring wine into little cups, and smoking dope and hash. Buzzed and pancaked to the earth, fans studied the festival's schedule, which was folioed in the middle of the program and inscribed in freehand on a grid using broad seventies script: 3 p.m. Roosevelt Sykes and Bonnie Raitt on Stage One; 5 p.m. Bukka White on Stage Six; and 7 p.m. Taj Mahal on Stage Three. On Saturday, John Prine – who would arrive at the festival dressed in blue denim jeans, shirt, and jacket – was scheduled to host a tribute to Hank Williams; Murray McLauchlan and David Bromberg would play and discuss the influences of Bob Dylan; a workshop called "The Oppression of Women in Song" would be led by Alice Seeger; and Bruce Cockburn would perform the late set on Sunday night. Cockburn had played the festival once before, in 1971. That year, he was asked by Estelle Klein to guard the backstage "stockade" while the governing area coordinator was on break. At one point, James Taylor – a surprise visitor in '71 – asked to be let in, and Bruce said no. "I just figured that, you know, rules were rules, and so I did what Estelle told me. He was very polite, but it was clear that he wanted in. It was also clear that I wasn't letting him. Finally, Lightfoot came up and kind of saved me. He said, 'You know, Bruce, I really think it would be okay if you let James Taylor into the artists' tent.'"

The performers of Mariposa '72 were a collection of the popular and the obscure, the difficult and the easy. At one end of the spectrum was Bonnie Raitt – freckled and twenty-three years old in 1972 – and Prine, then a fresh-faced American songwriter. If they weren't yet part of American musical history, they were certainly at the vanguard of the

From left to right: David Bromberg, John Prine, and John Allan Cameron at Mariposa, 1972

contemporary sound. Prine had recently tumbled across the radar of music fans, even though, just eighteen months prior, he'd been working as a mailman in Maywood, Illinois. The first review of his music came from film critic Roger Ebert after hearing him sing on open mic night at the Fifth Peg folk club. Of Prine's Mariposa shows, Bruce Cockburn recalls, "After the rumour started to circulate that Dylan might be coming to the island, people heard Prine's voice coming from another stage, and went to it, thinking it was Bob singing."

If Prine's shows were undoubtedly great, his time in Toronto would also produce many strange moments. Denise

Donlon, now the head of music programming at the CBC, remembered rescuing him out of a garbage can. "It appeared as if he'd gone in there head first," she said. Volunteer Honey Novick — an original member of the groundbreaking Canadian art collective General Idea — was given the task of minding John Prine. "He was absolutely blottoed that weekend," she remembered. "He was really fucked up, so I'm not surprised that he ended up in a garbage can. I don't know how he got his booze, or where — it was a dry festival — but he got it. He was notorious that way." On Sunday night, Novick took him to the Riverboat, where he was going to be introduced to the folk community. "I had to make sure that he didn't fall down or hurt himself and that he got back safely to the hotel," she said. "The thing that was special about John was that I trusted him, even in his drunkest state. I knew he wouldn't come on to me, and there seemed to be a silent communication between us, an understanding without words. He was happy-go-lucky, as well as gracious and jovial. When he finally got on stage that night, he was incredible."

In 1972, Bonnie Raitt was more quietly established than John Prine. By her late teens, she'd already played bottleneck guitar with Howlin' Wolf and Mississippi Fred McDowell, whom she met through her mentor, blues promoter Dick Waterman. Mariposa '72 was her first time in Canada. She travelled with her bass player, Freebo, and she was a presence most nights at the Executive Motor Hotel, leading jam sessions in one of the dark, pot-foggy rooms. During her early evening set on Saturday, the power was cut because of a rainstorm,

Bob Dylan and Leon Redbone at Mariposa, 1972

forcing her to seek shelter in one of the nearby tents. Most of the crowd dispersed, leaving a few dozen to wait out the show. Raitt gestured for them to join her under the canopy, where she sat down and played with Freebo while everyone listened, ringing out their clothes and shoes.

These contemporary songwriters were bookended by the spectre of Leon Redbone, who was as elusive as Raitt was available. For the Mariposa program, Redbone submitted a self-penned biography: "I was born in Shreveport, La. in 1910, and my real name is James Hokum. I wear dark sunglasses to remind me of the time I spent leading Blind Blake throughout the south, and I now live in Canada as a result of the incident in Philadelphia." Wikipedia tells us that Redbone's real name

— although it doesn't sound real — was Dickran Gobalian — and
that he was born in Cyprus. When editors of the program
asked for a photograph, he sent them a crumpled snapshot of
Dylan. In the mid-70s, a rumour started that Redbone was
actually Andy Kaufman in disguise — some also thought he was
Frank Zappa — despite earlier suspicions that he was actually
Bob Dylan's alter ego. Redbone has preserved the mystery surrounding his life and persona for over forty years. Or maybe
it's as Richard Flohil once told me: "Everyone tried so hard for
so long to figure out who Leon was that, eventually, a lot of us
just gave up."

Redbone wasn't the only eccentric at Mariposa. Louisiana
fiddler Doug Kershaw was there, too ("I remember having to
carry him across the mud so he wouldn't get his purple boots
dirty," said Flohil). Kershaw was Acadian by ancestry, and his
family settled in Tiel Ridge, where they lived for most of his
young life on a houseboat. His father was an alligator hunter
who taught him how to play the fiddle when he was five years
old. Legend has it that he used to sneak his father's instrument from the shelf when the old man went out fishing, and,
one day, he dropped and cracked it. When his dad got home,
he took Doug into a room and told him that he would avoid a
beating if he could play. Kershaw later called it his introduc-
tion to improvisation. His first ever appearance was at a local
bar called The Bucket of Blood, where he was accompanied
by his mother on guitar. A few years later, Kershaw's father
committed suicide, and well-documented are the musician's
struggles with sorrow and depression, as well as drugs and

alcohol. His song "Louisiana Man," was broadcast back to earth by the crew of Apollo 12, and, in 1975, he was married at the Houston Astrodome.

Kilby Snow was at Mariposa, as well. Described as "the Bill Monroe of the autoharp," Snow mastered the instrument at such a young age that he played at dances, socials, and bars when he was still well under the age of majority. The same was true of the Wareham Brothers, from Harbour Buffet, a small island in the middle of Placentia Bay, Newfoundland. Before coming to Mariposa, they'd never really had a proper gig before. Instead, it was mostly house parties and dances, which ended when Harbour Buffet was resettled by the Smallwood government to Arnold's Cove. To them, Mariposa must have seemed like paradise tenfold: trees and canals and pathways leading to the southernmost point of the city, which faced nothing but open water, except on a clear day and with a set of field glasses, when you can discern the faint outline of the Rochester shoreline. They were afforded a large and supportive audience in a big metropolitan city, many of whom were drawn to Mariposa the way museum-goers are drawn to a touring exhibit, grazing on musical history and absorbing dollops of new sounds. The same experience was likely even more surreal for the Dog Rib Indian dancers from Yellowknife, carver Saggiak Kumakooloo from Pangnirtung, and the Mississippi Fife and Drum Group. Because it was still the early seventies, travelling abroad meant going without many preconceived notions short of postcards (The Empire State Building: we climbed it!), a Sunday afternoon television program (*The*

Mystery of Machu Picchu), something somebody told you in a bar one night ("the women in Barcelona – they'll do anything!"), a disaster splashed on the front page of a supermarket tabloid (plane lost in the Bermuda Triangle), or a band who sounded like exactly where they came from (King Sunny Ade, Nigeria). The musicians may or may not have heard of Mariposa – or in some cases, Toronto – but it's not hard to think that what they found when they hit the grass was beyond anything they might have imagined.

As well as minding John Prine, Honey Novick was asked to make sure that the elderly Inuit folksingers were cared for. "It was the first time any of them had been out of the North," she said, "so, one afternoon, I decided to bring them into the city. I took them on the subway, which terrified them. They found the trains so fast, and even though it was a moderate weekend, temperature-wise, the heat was stifling to them. They were astounded by the city, by Yonge Street. We didn't understand each other, but we communicated the same way I'd communicated with a very drunken John Prine: through facial expressions and the occasional silent hand gesture. It's hard to know for sure what the impact of the weekend was on the elders, but, for me, it was an experience that ended up changing the course of my life. Our worlds were unfolding in strange and different ways, and we were right there in the middle of it."

Since this book is set in the folk realm of the sixties and seventies, it was only a matter of time before it intersected with someone named Skye, and so, early Friday morning, Skye Morrison arrived at Mariposa. It was her responsibility, along with a few others, to get the craft area going; setting up the tables, rigging the kilns, and making sure all of the artisans were where they were supposed to be, which, the night before, was scattered all over town.

"[My parents] were some of the original folkies," she told me. "When I was born, I was known as a 'red diaper baby,' being the child of left-leaning parents from Western Canada. When I was five years old, my mother and godmother brought Marian Anderson, the American opera singer, to the Macdonald Hotel in Edmonton – the old CN hotel – the first time a black person had ever been allowed in there. They had dinner and it was a huge news story. After we moved east, my folks took me to Mariposa when I was eight, and it became part of my cultural life. The folk music scene had lots of overtly political songs, but it was also a populist way of explaining the realities of the world. It was hard not to get something out of them, even at a very young age.

"Mariposa in '72 was still a lot more like what Newport would have been eight or ten years earlier. It maintained its integrity because of its devotion to traditional artists and to its ideology, which included craftspeople and artisans as well. It had an authenticity despite a changing world and changing music scenes, and those who ran it still believed that there could be a connection between music and people. Remember: the stages were one foot off the ground. Even though the musicians were held in very high regard and valued above all, they were presented on equal terms with the audience. Having gone to high school with Chris and Ken Whiteley, and known Joni Mitchell back when she was Joni Anderson, they were just people [to me]: extremely talented people. When they all returned to Mariposa in '72, it wasn't that big a deal because a lot of us thought, 'They came from here and here is where they're supposed to be.'"

From the beginning, Mariposa had tried to present the craft area and the artisans on equal terms, but they were always regarded as oddities at a music festival. They showed on the fringes of the festival site, even though what many of them were doing was as creative as the musicians themselves. In 1972, Bill Reid, the legendary Haida artist, carved there, and Norman Kennedy, the Scottish balladeer and master weaver, would perform Hibernian walking songs from the distant past. Shelly Fowler, who worked alongside Morrison, remembers: "The craft area had its own struggles. Putting on a concert is hard, but trying to get a dozen or more artisans set up with their tools and requirements was as challenging as anything going on on the stages. We had to get permission for the glassblowers, because they used heat, and it was a hassle, but we did it every year. There were also the raccoo potters. It was necessary for them to build a pit in the ground to fire their work with hot ashes, and we had to make sure the smoke went downwind. They also used dung for their fuel, and one time, they brought it over in big garbage bags. Of course, the sanitation guys on the island took it away. The responsibility fell to me to go and get it back. They were big guys and they'd been drinking and I had to ask them to go in and retrieve these bags of dung for me, which, after a difficult while, they finally did. We had to bring the torches, kilns, and potters wheels over to the island a few days before the festival opened, so it was more than just three days of work for us. What made the whole experience even more difficult was the fact that crafts-persons hadn't yet gained the respect or reputation that they have today. Jim Smith, the wooden toy-maker from Ottawa, had a wife who used to wear a T-shirt that said 'No I am not retarded' on it, because she was sick of being looked at as a second-class artist."

The native area and the craft area were next to each other, so there was a camaraderie between the presenters. Morrison remembers one night when the Labradorians and Newfoundlanders decided to stage a *ceili* (a Maritime social), and having to haul enormous heaters over to an area where, she said, "People were determined to make biscuits and par-tridgeberry jam for the party. It was a lot of trouble and a lot of work, but you did it because stuff like this happened at the festival that didn't happen anywhere else. Sure, you expected to party with Newfoundlanders in St. John's, but not in down-town Toronto. It had a transformative quality. Things hap-pened that weren't happening anywhere else in the world."

Gordon Klager recalls: "In between the headliners, my friends and I would watch all of the amazing traditional musi-cians; people like Jean Carignan, the legendary fiddler from Lévis, Quebec. He'd do workshops with Rufus Guinchard. They'd play a Quebecois tune, a Celtic tune, a Newfoundland tune, and then Jean would play something by Bob Wills, with whom he'd toured as a young man. It was incredible: all of this deep musical history coming alive right in front of you. It's not like it is today, when you can see traditional and folk musicians performing at most places at different times during the year. Back then, people wouldn't hire them to play normal clubs, and that's why Jean Carignan drove a cab. He couldn't make a living despite being an incredible musician. Mariposa was our one opportunity to see and hear them, and, in '72, you had these stars – these huge artists – hanging out and playing, as well."

While thousands were gathering on the isthmus for the first day of Mariposa, a report came over police radios that Donald Oag was in Ottawa. They'd found a car there, a '53 Chevy Nova that had been reported missing from Kingston on Wednesday morning. Oag's prints were on the steering wheel, and so were Thomas McCauley's, who'd been spotted on Bank Street. McCauley was the first prisoner ever to escape from Millhaven – it had happened months before the July jailbreak – and if police assumed that the two men were working together, they also assumed that Oag did the heavy lifting while McCauley, the elder of the two, plotted how to move forward. In the back seat of the Nova, two barrels had been found, "about sixteen inches long and sawed from a shotgun," according to police. Later that day, a man driving the same kind of vehicle and using a similar weapon had pulled up to the

Eastview Hotel in Vanier and robbed the clerk of $340. Police also reported that the body of a fifty-year-old farmer, Gabriel Lalande, had been found near Rockland, Ontario. The *Globe and Mail* reported that "police have not ruled out the possibility that the death may be connected to the escaped prisoners." The victim was discovered by his brother-in-law, Jean-Paul Guibord, who said that, when he opened the door to Lalande's home, "it looked like a real massacre. The room had been turned upside down. It was a real mess." An autopsy revealed that Mr. Lalande had died of strangulation. Mr. Guibord told reporters that his brother-in-law was very timid, but very strong, and "it would (have taken) more than one man to have done this to him." Lalande was found naked and lying on the floor near the bed. His hands and feet were tied with a clothesline and there was a rag stuffed in his mouth. Before disappearing into the night, one of the killers had torn a sheet from Lalande's bed, let it ripple in the air like the wings of a manta ray, and laid it over the victim's body.

Friday was Bastille Day in France. Thousands of people lined the Champs-Élysées to watch the annual parade. Men and women waved flags, sipped wine, and threw flowers. Vendors sold chestnuts and the cafes were overflowing. According to Reuters, the highlight of the event was the unveiling of a seventy-foot-long surface-to-surface missile with a range of nearly 3,000 kilometres. Its appearance, however, proved in-auspicious when the truck hauling the missile broke down in front of the crowd. Still, the weapon was massive as it lay in the shadow of the Eiffel Tower. It was designed to carry a 150-kiloton nuclear warhead, almost twice the size of the last French bomb. Authorities said that they needed this one tested, too. France would be the world's nuclear king. They would show the U.S.A. and Russia that, when it came to the muscle of war, this effete Gallic nation could stand next to them on the world's stage.

On Friday, Bobby Fischer must have surprised himself, although it's hard to know for sure, because it was clear that he was "sumashedski," a word that the park-bench players in Moscow used to describe the unhinged methods of the American challenger. Fischer kept pushing for new demands, even though it had been over twenty-four hours since he'd last sat across from Spassky and played. The latest demand was the most unreasonable: Fischer wanted to move rooms. He wanted the match to be squirrelled away in a small table-tennis room at the back of the hall, far from prying eyes and the hot threat of the TV camera lens, which, he said, were affecting his mindset as well as the integrity of the summit.

It was an outrageous demand coming from someone who, to the Russians, appeared incapable of dignity or sportsmanship. This is to say nothing of the logistics of the proposed move. The hall was spacious and beautiful and had been fitted to accommodate ticketed patrons, although it wasn't necessarily the patrons who were the source of Fischer's concern. It was still the television cameras, which the American saw as an Orwellian force working to corrupt the personal and interior nature of the game. He told organizers that he would only continue if either the television cameras were removed or the game shifted to the space behind the main stage at the back of the hall. The governing committee told him that this would be impossible, and then, like a magician well versed in the black arts, Fischer forced a wide creasing smile before producing a plane ticket for a flight departing that evening, non-stop Reykjavik to New York.

It's impossible to imagine any player or athlete in any sport today having a greater influence over their game than the TV networks who now pay untold billions for broadcasting rights. But that summer in Iceland, Fischer's insolence, temerity, cleverness, and arrogance towered above the match and its promoters, who'd worked tirelessly to stage it at a time when, diplomatically, the Americans and the Russians were locked in the Cold War. The organizers caved. They dragged everything into the table-tennis room, a single closed-circuit camera broadcasting images to the crowd in the hall. Fischer — delighted yet conciliatory, naturally — saw an opportunity, and he pounced. Soon after game three started, the American twice had Spassky in check, using a hostile pincer move to devour his middle pawn, leaving the Russian's king exposed. Spassky, his defeat in the game imminent, scraped his chair back and walked away. The Soviet delegation announced that they would be sending organizers a tersely worded letter of protest over the conditions of the new room, and threatened to quash the event. Two could play at this game of disgrace.

They were in the dock, wounded and wrecked. McTaggart told anyone who'd listen how the French sailors had assaulted him; how they'd climbed aboard the *Greenpeace III* after their ship had rammed it: a dozen angry soldiers versus Canada's badminton champion and his crew of two. McTaggart hadn't resisted, but the sailors raged anyway, and, at the end of it, the *Greenpeace III* and its crew had to be towed to Fiji for repairs. A British sailor took over command while McTaggart flew back to Vancouver to be treated at home. Before getting on his plane, he bought a newspaper and read what a lot of other people had read that day: the French had successfully detonated three blasts in the South Pacific. On the plane ride home, McTaggart's emotions brewed. He lay his head on his lunch tray for what seemed like an eternity, devastated and sick to his stomach. A few weeks later, however, he would open the newspaper to read another story about how a Christchurch scientist had detected radioactive fallout in New Zealand. The scientist said that, after extensive testing, iodine-131 had been found in a sample of milk taken on the west coast of the country's South Island. "Fission material," he called it. McTaggart would spend the next two years planning his return to the South Pacific. In 1974, he repaired his ship, sailed back to the atoll, and was rammed again. He was beaten worse. Beaten badly. But this time, McTaggart took photographs. The photos were smuggled and released to the press. McTaggart sued the French government, and there were marches: three or four that summer in Paris, demanding that the government stop doing what they'd been doing for years. When McTaggart's case was heard, the French court, in a landmark decision, ruled against their own government. The nuclear program fell to its knees. Finally, France ended its atmospheric nuclear testing, and the authorities vowed to leave Moruroa alone. McTaggart paused to celebrate, but by the time the decision came through, he had other things on his mind. Nuclear waste was flooding the oceans. Antarctica was being savaged by mining and oil exploration. And the whales. The whales needed help.

On Friday, Garth Douglas and his friend headed to Centre Island, arriving late at night. "When we got there," he said, "we realized straight away that Mariposa was sold out. We'd gone with the vague notion of something happening, and we wanted to be part of it." Douglas and his friend were both eighteen at the time. They stood on the lagoon shore opposite Algonquin Island with about three thousand other folks and noticed that a flimsy storm fence had been erected on the other side. It was a hot day, and the water looked cool and inviting. "Right then and there," remembered Douglas, "my friend, Lawrence, looked at me and I looked at him and we just dove into the water. I remember swimming for awhile and then reaching the other side. Looking behind me, I could see that a few hundred others had followed us into the water. We were the catalysts. One Mariposa official actually helped us over the fence. He said, 'Well, if you guys want to be in here so badly, who I am to keep you out?' In the afternoon we found a bag of abandoned ice-cubes. They were sitting in a bag under a tree. We passed them out to the folks around us, and going down, the notion hit us that they might have been laced with acid. Turned out, they were. We had a great day, heard some fabulous music, and enjoyed our illicit ramble immensely."

On Friday, the press release came via *Pravda*. It was announced in a two-inch column in the sports pages of the *Globe and Mail* that Team Russia would feature players named Kharlamov, Yakushev, Mikhailov, Petrov, Tretiak, Gusev, Blinov, Anisin, and others. They were funny names that no one associated with hockey. They were obscure and strange, and it was impossible for anyone to measure them with any weight. Still, Harry Sinden felt that he had to say something. "These Russians are better than any other Russian team," he told the press. "No one has asked me for a prediction, so I'll say it anyway: This will be a good series."

Rudolph Nuss heard Harry's quote on the radio of the taxi cab that was driving him home. Nuss was twenty-five. As a kid, he couldn't keep still. Thoughts jumped about him like skeet balls. His eyes jiggled and he chewed the insides of his mouth thinking three sentences and fourteen steps ahead of everyone else. Sitting in class proved impossible. To keep himself engaged during test papers, he'd make up stories or poems or imaginary rocket car schematics using every fourth letter of the questions written on the page, and after he'd done these things in his head, he'd leave just enough time to fill in just enough answers to give him just enough of a failing grade. Teachers held him back. Principals scolded and suspended him. He shredded through counsellors and frustrated tutors. His parents loved him hard, but no one knew if he was crazy and broken or brilliant, least of all them.

Everyone else was escaping from the prison that day, so, duh, of course he was going, too. While inside, he'd written letters home to his parents describing the roar of sounds to which the young incarcerate rose every morning: a symphony of septum-clanging snoring; the predictable and weary shuffling of the guards towards the cells; the morning clarion of the baton rattling across prison doors; the garbled protestations of formerly sleeping inmates and the guards swearing them awake; farting, creaking, yargling, belching, hacking, and more farting; and the grumbling echo of the men's defeated lives as they filled the empty, grey hallways. Once Rudolph was outside, it wasn't his legs or fear or heart rate that propelled him, but his imagination. It carried him farther than any other inmate. Most of the prisoners had made it to neighbouring counties, but Rudolph went beyond that.

Police thought about looking for him at his home in Niagara-on-the-Lake, but it was preposterous to think that he could have made it that far, not with all of the roadblocks and provincial and federal authorities prowling the depths of the bush from Pickering to Sydenham. But they found no trace of Rudolph in the immediate area, and, for a moment, some wondered whether he'd been murdered by another inmate, but who would have had the time and what would they have done with the body? The OPP were assigned to the case. At first, it was like chasing a ghost. Then they checked his parents' home in Niagara, just in case the convict had done what any fugitive in his right mind wouldn't have done. But Rudolph wasn't like any other fugitive. And whether he was in his right mind was a matter of debate. The policemen knocked on the door. He was in his room, reading or building or composing. He came down. He surrendered without a fight.

On Friday, the government announced that, despite pressure from fans, it would not take the initiative to persuade NHL owners to let Bobby Hull play for Team Canada. Trudeau shrugged hands-in-vest as he told the press: "We do not wish the collapse of the series over one player." This triggered a shitstorm of public revolt, plummeting Trudeau even deeper in public opinion polls. The Civil Service Association of Alberta accused Hockey Canada of pandering to the NHL. Then, Manitoba tourism minister Larry Desjardins sent a telegram to health minister John Munro protesting Hull's exclusion. Before long, Hockey Canada's Phil Reimer had resigned as governor of the organization and billboard magnate

Claude Neon – a real shit disturber – announced he was putting up over 300 billboards across the country: TO HULL WITH RUSSIA (the signs were erected overnight). In Alberta, 23,000 people marched in the streets of Edmonton protesting the WHA player's absence; the long-hairs at CHUM radio in Toronto and CJAD in Montreal organized a series of listener petitions; and hundreds of others telephoned and sent letters to Munro's office, one of them accusing the NHL of "raping Canadian hockey." CBLT television interviewed a man on the street – Leng Pap Jr. was his name – who called Hockey Canada's gaffe "the boob of the century." The Russians said nothing. Then, just before Friday drifted into Saturday, a short message came over the wire from beyond the Kremlin wall: "It makes no difference to us whether Bobby Hull plays or not."

All of this made Harry's head hurt. Sure, he wanted Bobby Hull on his team, but there were other things to worry about. Like Orr. Nobody wanted to talk about Orr: how he could barely skate on those goddamned knees; how it hurt when he stood up to piss. You think those WHA fly-by-nighters never waved a mill' or two or three or four in front of Orr's nose? Hull bit, and, because he bit, he'd created a goddamned mess that Harry didn't need. Orr was loyal to the Bruins and he was loyal to his fans. You don't think Hull pissed off the people of Chicago when he left for goddamned Winnipeg? He thought he could do anything, but he was wrong. Now people wanted to get goddamned Trudeau on the goddamned case, but he was as useless as tits on a bull.

There was something else nagging at Harry. It was a feeling he was loathe to explain to his friends or associates lest it come out sounding like some sort of inarticulate lunacy. Besides, the nature of the series demanded that he remain square-shouldered and resolute in his determination and leadership. Any sense of doubt would be considered a weakness, and damned if he was going to give the Russians reasons to believe that they could penetrate the famous Canadian resolve.

It might have been pathos, though Harry probably didn't know the word. Harry's feelings were triggered by a sense of change. And what was changing was everything. In the aftermath of the 1972 Summit Series, hockey would, over the following twenty years, be remade, disfigured, eviscerated, transformed, prettied, denuded, sweetened, corrupted, and liberated: all of these things. When Sinden and his team found themselves down by two goals in the third period of game eight in Moscow, people assume that the reason they were able to soldier their way to the slimmest of victories was because they were honouring the legacy of the players' families and cities and their common flag. And they were, in a way. But what they were also doing was, subconsciously or otherwise, trying to hold on to the last vestiges of life as they knew it: helmetless three-minute shifts and spare-tire waistlines; summer training sessions of water skiing and grilled steaks in Muskoka; hair grown to whatever length they wanted and backchecking at their leisure; ultra-violent on-ice behaviour that caused no national symposia or interdisciplinary committees; and seventeen years serving the same team in the same city. But the

moment the players of Team Canada '72 stepped on the goddamned stage of that goddamned hotel in that goddamned
city on that goddamned stinking hot Wednesday afternoon,
everything was already different, and even if the Russians lost
every game, which Harry knew they would not, the past was
gone. How fast it would disappear, or how much it would
change, no one knew. Sure, maybe players would cut their hair
a little. Maybe no one would ever be called Battleship or
Hound Dog or Old Elbows or Spinner or Crazy Eyes anymore.
Maybe white boards would be splashed with adverts for soft
drinks and car dealerships and maybe glorious old buildings
would tumble for new glassy arenas named after banks and
airlines and something called jobbing.com. Maybe games
would be lengthened by twenty to thirty minutes because of
endless time outs and maybe someone would come along and
break a few old records. And maybe the fighting would dim, if
by degrees. But there's no way anyone would ever speak any
language other than English or French in an NHL dressing
room. And there's no way – none – that games would ever be
settled by what some Europeans leagues were already doing in
1972: players taking breakaways one after the other to decide
games that ended in ties. Harry shook his head as he walked
into the hotel bar. Hockey would change and it would change
huge. But Christ, thought Harry, it would never get that weird.

On Friday at Mariposa, Roberta Richards had to get Bukka
White his medicine. This sometimes meant actual medicine,

but sometimes it meant other things, too. "On the Friday of most festivals, Bukka like to tell people that, on Sunday, it would be his forty-ninth birthday," said Roberta, who now lives with her family in Guelph, Ontario. "Of course, it was his birthday at every festival. Then he'd say, 'I'm not asking for gifts, you know, but if you choose to bring me something, I like bourbon.' By the end of the festival, there was enough booze to get an army drunk."

Estelle Klein had entrusted Roberta with the festival's blues acts, having promoted blues artists ever since she got into the business as a sixteen-year-old promoter. Roberta "practically grew up in a trunk." One of her grandfathers was a theatre promoter in Toronto, while the other was a promoter in New York City. Her Toronto grandparents promoted shows with performers ranging from Jimmy Crawford to Duke Ellington, who often stayed at their Bathurst and College home because of bigoted local hotel policies. After her grandparents moved to the deep South, Roberta visited them often, and it was during these trips that her musical consciousness started to expand. "One day, I saw a poster advertising a show for Rompin' Ronnie Hawkins in Arkansas," she said, "and I begged my grandfather to take me. He told me that my grandma would kill him if she found out – I was underage at the time – but he took me anyway, hiding me behind the cigarette machine. This was my upbringing in music, and when I got back to Toronto, the folk scene was kicking in around the clubs in Yorkville. I never quite got it. A lot of people in Yorkville were writing songs about lost loves and their dog dying and their truck breaking down, and I felt that they had a very rigid agenda. They wrote downer songs about how bad everything could be, but I'd met rural blues people, and I knew how bad things were. What these folk singers were singing about wasn't bad. There are work songs that are hopeful in the face of sadness or tragedy, but a lot of folk music of the time just didn't clue into that."

Roberta started to book bands in Toronto, focusing on the blues. "When I first met Bukka White, he told me that his name was Booker T. Washington White, but that I should call him 'Big Daddy,'" she said. "Roosevelt Sykes was very sweet, too. He was religious, and when the others would go off for their 'medicine,' he would just bow his head and say grace. Playing the festival was a huge adjustment for these musicians because they were old, they'd had hard lives, and it wasn't easy for them to get around. Besides, since everybody got paid the same amount of money, it was hard for them to make what they felt — and I felt — they deserved. So we'd book them an extra show while they were in town. The hospitality often left them wanting, too, so I'd take them out for dinner to the Underground Railroad [an old restaurant in Toronto named after the passageway by which American slaves fled to Canada] and they would dig in. They understood the significance of the restaurant's name. I sat there listening for hours as they talked about their families, telling stories of slavery."

Ken Whiteley, who'd gone to his first Mariposa in 1964, remembers: "It was the old blues guys who blew my mind. In 1964, Sonny Terry and Brownie McGhee were supposed to play, but nobody told them that the festival had moved [from

Orillia to Toronto], so they never made it. Mississippi John Hurt was on the bill and so was the Reverend Gary Davis. Then Dick Waterman, who discovered John Hurt — as well as Bonnie Raitt, who was there in '72 — had also found Skip James in a hospital bed eighteen days before the event, so he brought him down, too. They were going to play Newport, so he wanted them to get their feet wet. In the dugout of the stadium [Maple Leaf Stadium, the site of that year's festival], I watched John Hurt and Reverend Davis meet each other for the first time, talking and trading songs. They were so excited to be in each other's company. I heard Skip James sing, 'I'd rather be the devil/than be my woman's man,' and it made such an impact that I went home singing it. My parents looked at me like I was crazy. I was thirteen years old."

Roberta recalls: "I developed a friendship with Arthur 'Big Boy' Crudup, who wrote 'That's All Right,' which was the first hit for Elvis [Crudup was allegedly discovered by producer Lester Melrose while living in a packing crate]. He was eighty-nine years old in 1972 and had been married for fifty-eight years. After his wife passed away, I remember him sitting at a picnic bench and playing for my kids, who loved him. He turned to my husband, David, and said, 'You know, I've got this great idea. I wrote a song way back in the forties called "Roberta," and, well, you know, I love this Roberta,' he said, meaning me. He told Dave, 'Because I love her, I want to marry her.' Dave said, 'Well, if she says she wants to marry you, that's fine,' so Arthur leaned over to me and said, 'Roberta, will you marry me?' I was pretty sure that he was joking, but then he said, 'Listen, I have this little house in Virginia. I have a rowboat and I like to go fishing for catfish. So if you marry me and come to Virginia, I can fish and Dave can play guitar and sing with me and it will be great.' I asked him what I'd do, and he said, 'Well, you can clean the fish and do the gardening and take care of the house. And the kids can run around and have a great time.' I realized that while the part about me marrying him was sort of a joke, the idea of us going with him to keep him company wasn't. He actually thought it's what all of us would do and that we'd go on and live happily ever after. He died a few years later, at ninety-one. But that was his idea of a perfect life. It doesn't seem bad at all."

On Friday, Colin Linden, his mom, and his brother collected their bedrolls and blankets and headed to the lake. They were going to Mariposa. "I'd studied the program for every other Mariposa," he remembered. "I'd read all of the bios, the ads; memorized the clubs, the record companies, the radio stations. I spotted an ad for the Fiddler's Green, and I started hanging out there, seeing tons of musicians, a lot of whom were at the festival. When we went over on the ferry, there were already tons of people jamming on the boat. My show was at an open stage – stage three, to be exact – and it was the greatest day of my life, to that point. It was the first time I'd ever performed in front of an audience and my eyes were opened to so many things. The morning started with a dulcimer workshop with Bruce Cockburn, but before that, I remember seeing him sitting at a picnic table. I went over and introduced myself; he still remembers our encounter to this day. Later on, there was a blues workshop with Bonnie Raitt, Bukka White, and Lonnie and Ed Young, who were part of a fife and drum ensemble from Mississippi playing the strangest, most beautiful music I'd heard: marching band tunes from the rural South played on instruments the players had made themselves.

"There were a lot of connections made that day; among everyone, and for myself, in a personal sense. Before my set – which was hosted by Chick Roberts – I was warming up on a little tree stump when a guy came up and started talking to me. He wanted to know who I was and where I came from and what I was all about. He asked when I was playing and I told him, and then he said that he was going to come and watch. I didn't think anything of it, but when I looked out in the crowd, there he was: John Prine, who'd just put out his first album. I told the crowd what I'd vowed to say: 'When I left New York City two years ago, I was ten years old. Now I'm sixty-two, so I've grown fifty-two years in two years. If that ain't the blues, I don't know what is.' After my set, Chick said that I should play the next day, but I didn't want to come across being too greedy or anything. But he encouraged me; he told me that, no, it was okay. So I did. The stage was emceed by John Allan Cameron, the great Cape Breton songwriter. Afterwards, my brother and I were wandering around just as the sun was starting to set. And that's when we came across Lightfoot and the Goods, sitting at a picnic table, just playing.

"The thing that was great about Mariposa was that it was an environment that was cool enough for all of those stars to be at, and to hang around, but it was also cool enough for a kid like me to play. For a second, those two realities coexisted, and it was rare and very special. There was a very clear connection being made between musicians at every level, whether you were a beginner, or whether you were signed to a label and had made hit records. Being on a small island helped all of that, of course, and being on a small island just off the shore of Toronto factored into whatever magic was at play. Some dyed-in-the-wool Mariposa-ites thought that having these stars ruined it for everybody, and that always sort of saddened me. There was something that was very self-defeating about that attitude, and, as a result, the next year Mariposa went out of its way to make sure that no one famous showed up, and really, that no one would have any fun. Still, the Winnipeg Folk Festival was hatched in '74 because of what Mariposa did. Same with Festival of Friends and Hamilton in '76, and the Home County Festival in London. They put festivals on the map in Canada. It was a true beginning for me, and for countless others."

LETTER IN WHICH I ASK YOU ABOUT DYLAN, AND IN WHICH I GO ON A TRIP UP NORTH

Gord, the good times finally came in 1965. Every singer wants to explode, and Gord, you exploded. Albert Grossman was managing you, and he got you a record deal with United Artists. Lots of people covered your songs – hit songs – before anyone outside of Toronto knew who you were. You were covered by Marty Robbins ("Ribbon of Darkness"), George Hamilton IV ("Steel Rail Blues"), Peter, Paul and Mary, and Johnny Cash. Hey, Gord: what's it like to be covered by Johnny Cash? I guess it's like being covered by Gordon Lightfoot, which has happened a few times before. Harry Dupe tells this story: "I was at Massey Hall on May 6, 1998. Gord was introducing a new song, written, he said 'by my friend, Steve, and I've heard it played lots around the bars of Muskoka. It's called "I Used to Be a Country Singer."' Gord plays it and the response is really good. After it's done, he looks down at the crowd, and he finds Steve, sitting near the front of the stage.

He says to Steve, 'Hey, good one, pal! I think they like it!' Then Gord says to the crowd: 'Jeez, I don't know how I'm going to follow that.' And the band kicks into 'Wreck of the Edmund Fitzgerald.'"

Soon, people were going nuts for you. You were named Folksinger of the Year, beating Joni, Ian and Sylvia, and that weird poet with the enormous schnozz, the Montrealer, Leonard Cohen. The American Society of Composers, Authors and Publishers named "Ribbon of Darkness" the best country song of the year. Your music tapped into the very essence of the Canadian soul at a time when Canadians were just trying to figure out who they were and what they were about. You gave your people a voice. You gave them a musical hero.

Your friend, and mine, Dan Hill said: "There was a time in Canada when people would say, for instance, 'Well, Pierre Berton is a really bright guy, but he's no Norman Mailer,' or 'He'd get torn up if he debated William F. Buckley.' But in music, you couldn't say that about Lightfoot. You couldn't say, 'Well, he's good for a Canadian' because he was the first musician from here to be very highly regarded internationally. People don't realize the effect now, and it's hard, because, there are tons of Canadian stars. But back then, there weren't, and to have him achieve at such a high level was very socially and culturally important."

Everyone talks about how you provided a cultural bridge: how you bridged town to city, country music to folk, folk to pop, old to new, square to hip, Canadian music to hit radio, and, later, the sixties sound to the seventies. Even now, when people see you or hear you, they see the past being bridged to the present. Stompin' Tom and Rush are still around, sure, but you predated all of them. And while you're still going, you're no museum piece. You played seventy shows in 2009. I know this because you punched Geddy Lee in the arm at a SOCAN dinner and asked him, in a growly, pirate voice (at least that's the voice that Geddy used when he told the story): "How many shows d'ja do last year?" He said something like "a hundred," and you thumbed your chest and told him how many you'd done. Geddy was impressed by that, and so am I.

In 1967, people started calling you "Canada's Bob Dylan" – even "The New Dylan" – but I'm not sure that impressed you (for the record, I've always considered you to be more like "Canada's Bob Marley," a person whose music translates wherever it's played, but also maintains a very strong sense of place). The term "The New Dylan" has always been a bit of a curse, and, these days, it's a little shopworn. Anyone who ever sang a song through their septum about a one-eyed pirate making love to a peg-legged gypsy while somewhere a war is happening that shouldn't be has been called the new Dylan. Anyone who's ever worn a proletariat cap and shuffled along with their hands stuffed in the pockets of their plaid bomber jacket? Yup: the new Dylan. And anyone who's ever written an elegy about injustice set to three chords and a bridge in either A minor, B minor, or D minor and named it after something they saw in whatever room they happened to be sitting in – "Ballad of a Withered Potted Plant" or "Musings of a Budgie in a Wrought-Iron Cage" – then given that song a random number – "Tiger-Stripe Hoop Skirt #327" or "Sitting on the Warm Banquette of an Old Winnebago #65" – has been called the same.

Lebanese folksinger Marcel Khalifé has been called the new Dylan. So has Cuba's Carlos Verela. So was Donovan Leitch, but we all know how that turned out. Jean Ferrat of France used to be the new Dylan, and so were Steve Forbert, Bruce Springsteen, Loudon Wainwright III, Arlo Guthrie, and John Prine. Bob's youngest son, Jakob, has also been called the new Dylan. Biologically, this isn't wrong.

One afternoon, my friend, Dave, who plays with hockey-punk band The Zambonis, was hanging out in a Vegas parking lot. He was attending the Guess Jeans convention, being a garment merchant in his other life. Both Neil Young and Bob Dylan were scheduled to play the company's closing night party; reports had them earning upwards of one million dollars each for their appearance. A small figure wearing a parka with the hood funnelled over his face passed Dave, who immediately recognized the figure as Dylan. "Hey Bob, how are you doing?" he asked. Dylan turned around and said, "I don't know you, man. Suck a dick!" I've told this story a lot, and, years later, it was told back to me at a party. Another story: Dylan, wanting to fire a member of his band, asked him to go out and find the sheet music for "White Christmas." When he returned, the person at the studio told him that, he was sorry, but this was Bob's way of relieving a musician of his duties. A third story: two winters ago, the people who live in Neil Young's boyhood home in Winnipeg noticed a car parked outside their house. The driver — a wraith in a black windbreaker and jeans — knocked on their door and asked if he could look around for awhile. The couple said he could, but by the time they realized it was Dylan, the singer was gone.

My friend and bandmate Don Kerr has done lots of important things. But one evening, Bob Dylan mentioned him on his radio show, so, although I wouldn't encourage it, you can shoot him now. The filmmaker Bruce McDonald has never met Bob Dylan, but telling a story about Bob Dylan has made him all the more important to those who measure the worth of others in such terms. The story isn't actually his; it's Gina Gershon's, the actress. One summer in Los Angeles, Gina decided to take boxing lessons. She was having a great time and improving her skills before her coach told her that she should probably spar with someone to see how far she'd come along. This sounded okay to her, and so the next day she climbed into the ring to find a fellow of comparable weight and height warming up on the ropes. After the bell dinged, she moved into the middle of the ring, at which point Dylan, scrunched into his headgear, came into view. Gina hit him anyway.

I've seen Dylan in concert once and he was terrible. It happens. No band or singer or musician is above bad performances. The show was at the Air Canada Centre and we were sitting a few seats away from Hurricane Carter, about whom Dylan wrote "Hurricane," which helped secure Carter's release from prison. Carter used to live a few blocks away from me in Toronto, and he kept his Christmas lights up year-round. He had enormous calves and wore a straw hat and wire-rimmed glasses. He seemed like a good guy, although I never watered my sidewalk around him. One neighbour who did was upbraided by the old boxer, who exhibited the kind of temper one might expect from someone who'd once hit people for a living.

Not even watching Hurricane Carter watching Bob Dylan sing "Hurricane" was enough to save the show that I saw. At one point, Bob paused whatever song he was singing to play a grating three-note riff on his guitar over and over again before putting the guitar down and reaching for his harmonica, upon which he continued the riff. This went on for five, ten minutes. Bob started each song singing incomprehensibly, and then, once the crowd figured out what song it was, they applauded

Bob, and the church of Bob, at Mariposa, 1972

out of respect. Of course, the next day's reviews were glowing. When it comes to Dylan, the Church of Bob will last well after the great songwriter is gone, no matter what kind of music he produces in his remaining years.

Since I was a hardrock album rat in the mid-seventies, Dylan's music was lost on me. His best music was probably behind him, and, as a result, I found records like *Street Legal* and *Slow Train Coming* confounding. Although these recordings captivated my stoner cousins, who were old enough to have experienced the first effect of his voice, I shrugged because they weren't *Wings Over America* or *Ummagumma* or *Houses of the Holy*. Because of my age, I wasn't able to comprehend what it meant to hear "Like A Rolling Stone" or "Masters of War" or "It's All Over Now, Baby Blue" pealing out of an AM radio or car stereo or steel-ribbed jukebox at a time when rock and roll radio featured songs about cars named after horses played by bands named after spacecraft. I'm not sure whose idea it was to start "Like a Rolling Stone" with a single snare shot – the effect is like a gavel strike, calling the listener to attention – but it's a brilliant beginning, more so because of the half-beat of silence that occurs before the band falls into it like bodies launched off a cliff. One can only imagine how it sounded when first released: a generation shocked alive by the full and glorious intensity of its words and music, despite the appearance of both a parrot and Siamese cat in the lyrics. This is to say nothing of Dylan's relentless harmonica, which sounds like what happens when you risk throwing those two creatures together in one song.

Dylan has played in Toronto lots of times. Like you, he's been on the CBC, too, strolling with his guitar through a fake log-cabin set built by men who came from small towns in Europe and who lived on Concord and Montrose and Crawford Street, working class neighbourhood men who probably saw Dylan as some kind of braying, unbathed, over-sexed, and talentless urchin not fit to scrape your boot heel, Gord. To them, you were a man's man, your piney tenor evoking character and resolve and an honest work ethic, while Dylan was a big-city fraud who played dress-up and sang in a language you'd have to be stoned to understand. In a way, they weren't wrong. Dylan was a folksinging kabuki — big sunglasses, mushroom afro, ridiculous nose, skinny jeans, beetle-stabber boots — and to think that he'd never played the part would be to misunderstand the very idea of mass entertainment, which is what Dylan was, and is, and continues to be. But for men who'd struggled to survive, let alone work, let alone work in a strange town with weird food and tasteless beer, the very idea of entertainment is heavy with suspicion, even though Dylan had sung about them, too, on *John Wesley Harding* and *Another Side of Bob Dylan* and *Highway 61 Revisited*. Still, you had a greater resonance because you've always been more song than entertainment. You never pancaked your face with makeup, or made videos (Dylan made the first, and arguably the best, for "Subterranean Homesick Blues"). Back in the fifties and sixties, working men distrusted freaks who sang about dope and war. Sure, Dylan was Dylan and he had hit records here, too. But he wasn't you. Nobody was.

You loved Dylan's music. I know this because Al Mair told me that you were a "110 per cent Dylan fan." From a distance, the feeling appears mutual, although as Cathy Evelyn Smith says in her book — which you should probably not read — whenever you guys hung out, the occasion was fraught with tension and uncertainty. There's a story about you meeting Dylan before Newport, but it sounds as if it was born from the Church of Bob, and, as a result, it can't be entirely trusted. The story goes that Albert Grossman introduced you to him, and that you conspired to hang out one night in New York City. Someone suggested you play a little pool. Someone (probably Dylan) might have said:

-Hey, man, you any good at pool? Cause I am, and I need something to chew on.

Then someone else (probably you) might have said:

-Yeah, sure, pool. Sounds good.

-But you can play, right?

-Sure I can play.

-Whaddya shoot, Gord?

-Whaddya mean what do I shoot?

-You know, what's your handicap?

-Oh. Um. I dunno. Maybe an eight?

-An eight? Jeezus. Even Van Ronk's a six. You sure you're only an eight?

-Well, maybe a seven. On a good night.

-Well, Gord. Here's hoping you're right.

Of course, you might have said none of this. Maybe Grossman brought you into his office and did all of the talking.

Maybe he brokered the evening, brokered the game. Maybe you said nothing during the meeting, being, by reputation, a quiet fellow. Maybe you just sat there and stared at Bob. After all, you'd been playing his songs for years. Maybe he liked it, this idolatry. Actually, not maybe. And not "liked." Dylan loved it. It's part of who he was and is. Which is not to say that he didn't admire your music. He did, and he does. I'm just saying.

In Maynard Collins' book, he describes how badly you played that night, how your inadequacies as a snookerist were laid bare.

-That's no seven handicap, Gord! That's maybe a nine or ten at best!

You might not have cared that you lost to Dylan – losing to him was something that musicians on every level did every day – but Collins says that "after the game, Gord went on to become a very good pool player." So maybe you did care. Or maybe Collins is simply channelling the Church of Bob. Or maybe losing to Dylan was a humiliation you simply could not stand, and, as I write this, you still harbour a dream of beating Dylan, that arrogant little flop-headed bastard from northern Minnesota, in a rematch, before harpooning your cue through his stomach.

Maybe, like Donovan in *Don't Look Back,* you were fed into the jaws of the great artist, the highly-driven and competitive folk-rock legend relishing every moment. Maybe he cackled when you missed a shot. Maybe he made fun of your clothes – your jeans, plaid shirt, and shoes – and then maybe he mocked the way you spoke:

-That shot was far "ooot," man. It was far "ooot!"

Or maybe he leaned against a plywood wall bathed in
Rolling Rock neon with his arm around the waist of a fine-
boned Vassarite slumming it in the trenches. Maybe he
howled with delight as you missed the pocket. Maybe you
ambled over to your date – who, Grossman would have insisted, should be a lower-rent Vassarite, maybe a diminutive
C-list actress; Selma Jean or something. Or maybe you
missed the shot on purpose, fighting your competitive impulses. Maybe you lost so that you could make your hero
happy. Or maybe you lost because you are Canadian. Because
you are nice.

But I don't know.

You won't talk to me.

At this point, Gord, I should do something that it is required
in biographies. I should serve the interests of readers who are
going to want to know about the mundane particulars of
your life. For instance, some people will want to know that
1) you like to shower wearing latex gloves so your calluses
won't soften (it's a weird image, thinking of you doing that);
or 2) you like to collect CHUM Charts (I read that on the
CHUM Chart site); or 3) you were asked to play at The Last
Waltz, but you refused because "I didn't feel I had the confidence to do it," (*Seattle Weekly*) even though you were there
at Winterland to say goodbye to The Band; or 4) your mother
once told the press that, when you were a kid, you used to

sing to yourself for an hour before you fell asleep; or 5) the songwriter, Phil Ochs, wrote his famous song, "Changes," while hanging out in your place on Admiral Street, where you lived with Brita; or 6) you annotate and construct all of your own songbooks; or 7) a famous actor who was sleeping with Cathy Smith used to belittle you by calling you "Footsie," and who once, after shagging Cathy in your hotel room, charged champagne and caviar in your name; or 8) you acted in a film called *Harry Tracy, Desperado;* or 9) you invested your money in apartments and plazas and now have over a gajillion dollars to your name; or 10) you record most of your song ideas on a cassette recorder, often while you're sitting around watching the Leafs play (you've done a lot of estimable things, Gord, but finding inspiration in the godawful Leafs might be your greatest achievement). Now, all of these things are interesting, sure, but I'm not sure that they tell anyone very much about who you are or why I'm even writing about you in the first place. I mean, if someone were to write a literary portrait of me, knowing that I sleep on the left side of the bed or refuse to acknowledge the sovereignty of the republic of Liechtenstein (I made that one up; I actually have nothing against Liechtenstein), you wouldn't really know who I am, not exactly. These details help illuminate the outline of a person, but rarely do they expose the person's true heart and soul, if these things can be exposed at all. Imagining you snapping on your gloves before climbing into the shower is an interesting image, I guess, but, in the end, it's only one frame, only one shot. It might be the only thing that some people remember after reading this book, and that's okay, too. I can't control that, but it doesn't mean that I'm going to stop trying to learn more.

Apart from the minutiae, there are the stories. Stories say a lot, and sometimes they say too much. Sometimes stories clarify things, but they complicate, too. One story will say one thing, and another story will say something that contradicts that story. It's maddening, but it's not dull. Sometimes, while writing this book, I wished it was about Jim down the street who, you know, gets up at seven o'clock every day and then goes to work and on Saturdays he takes his son to hockey practice and every third Friday he plays cards with his old university buddies and he smokes three joints and drinks four beers during the game and, on those weekends when he's pretty wrecked after coming home from cards, his wife, Janice, takes the kids to their Saturday activities so that Jim can sleep in and sometimes walk around naked with his schwang hanging out and pretty soon it's Sunday and he's back at work on Monday and the cycle all repeats itself. But unlike you, Jim never hung out with Dylan or wrote "Canadian Railroad Trilogy." So, while Jim has the occasional story told about him — like the time he accidentally put out a bonfire by vomiting — these stories are few and far between. And while Jim is a good guy, he's also kind of boring. Which you are not.

Not knowing you, Gord, I asked people for some stories. One person wrote to say that "if you want to ruin everyone's impression of their beloved Canadian music hero, then print all of the stories that people have about him. It'll expose him as the total drunken jerk that he is." But that isn't the case, at least not entirely. Here are some stories, each one very different from the next. I'll end this section with these stories, and then we'll move on. Sound okay? I just have to say: I'm having fun writing this book, at this point, anyway. It doesn't happen often: fun, that is, at least not while writing. Writing is a total pain in the ass. It's work. It's cracking rocks mixed in with the occasional moment where the heavens open and the prose explodes. But I've been lucky this time. Not to flatter, but maybe it's the subject. I dunno. I'm not blowing smoke. Okay, well, maybe I am, just a little. In any case, here are the stories. Maybe you shouldn't read them. But maybe you're just so swept up in this narrative, you can't help yourself (hee hee).

When my mom was a kid, she got her picture taken with Gordon and was on the cover of the Brantford Expositor. *Apparently, he was a real jerk, but they're both smiling in the picture. So my mom thinks he's a big faker.*
AMELIA CHESTER

I was a young girl in high school and totally in love with Gordon Lightfoot. My favourite song was "Pussywillows Cat-Tails," and so I saved up some money and a girlfriend and I bought tickets to his show at Massey Hall. We brought him a bouquet of, yup, pussywillows and cat-tails, and put them on stage with a note asking him to play it for us. He came out on stage kind of drunk and read our note and said, aloud: "I hate that fucking song." We were devastated. Somebody noticed our tears and we were invited backstage

to meet him and get his autograph. He apologized to us and gave me his empty whiskey bottle. I still have it. Every time I hear that song I laugh and wonder if Gordon Lightfoot still hates it.
MARCY BERG

Gordon Lightfoot is the grumpiest, most stuck-up, coldest, unapproachable, chauvinistic, miserable old bastard I've ever worked with. I'm a man, so I got on his good side. If you're a woman, he's got one use for you and then you can leave.
TREVOR WEEKS

Gordon Lightfoot is basically a nice guy from the country, if a little insecure that he came from the country.
RICHARD FLOHIL

About 1970 or so, I lived in the Soo. My dad brought me across the ditch to Sault, Michigan, to see Gord play. He was late by about an hour. When he finally showed up, he came out hammered, cussing all of the Americans in attendance, saying he'd never play again in the U.S.A.
MIKE SEVERIN

Everybody always wanted a piece of Gord and it was hard because there were no Canadian stars back then. Now, there are fifteen Nelly Furtados, but back in the sixties, there was Lightfoot and there was Lightfoot. His was an unusual career choice, too, so there was even more pressure. We all know that he has suffered from depression, and that alcohol is a symptom of depression; of filling

the void. There are a lot of creative artists who have demons. You combine the incredible pressures of stardom and the fact that everybody else is doing all of this wacky stuff; you put those things together, and suddenly, you're doing everything under the sun. Creativity is a way of dealing with it, but after awhile, Gord, I think, hit this perfect storm of anxiety and pressure. That's where the self-destructive stuff comes from, and because it was happening in Canada, it registered faster. There was no one else to sensationalize. He was right here, growing up with us.
DAN HILL

Once, I had to doorstep him at his house on the Bridle Path. I rang the bell and he opened the door in an undershirt and pair of jogging pants pulled up to his waist looking like a stooped but kindly old man. I actually said, "Are you Gordon Lightfoot?" He conceded that he was and let me in. The house was depressingly bare of furniture (his wife had just left him) apart from the study at the front of the house that was filled with music, equipment, instruments, and overflowing ashtrays. Then he said he had his manager on the phone and that he wanted to speak to me. When he handed me the phone the manager told me in no uncertain terms to get the fuck out: no interviews. He then very apologetically showed me the door. By the time I got back to the newsroom there was a message on my office voice mail. "Hi, Leah, it's Gordon. Could you please call me?" The next day I went to Massey Hall and he gave me a full interview followed by a private performance of "If You Could Read My Mind." Pure magic.
LEAH McLAREN

I was fortunate to have first met Gordon in August 1979. He had just finished performing at Ravinia Festival in Chicago, and because it was pouring (this being an outdoor venue), a few people were waiting inside the pavilion for the deluge to stop before heading back to their cars. After sitting there for about forty-five minutes, I happened to glance back at the stage and my jaw fell open. Gordon himself was walking directly to where a group of fans were standing. He began chatting with them and signing autographs. I was lucky enough to meet him and have my picture taken with him. He was kind and gracious and even though he was in the midst of what he now describes as being "a very bad period" in his life, I saw no evidence of anything other than a brilliant performer who generously took time to meet with fans and pose for pictures.

LAURA STOUT

When I was stuck in a rotten apartment in St. James Town, I went for a summer walk and saw a St. James Town Festival schedule taped in the window of the community centre. Among the bake sales and face painting, it said, "4:30 p.m.: Gordon Lightfoot." I figured that it couldn't be what it said. Sure enough, Gord showed up, still a little thin and frail, and played three or four songs for free, out of the goodness of his heart. One was "Black Day in July." Best Canadian moment since I helped Stompin' Tom carry his beer to his car.

MICHAEL BOWLES

The thing about Lightfoot is that he maintained his folk credibility as well as being big. He was both good and big, which isn't necessarily very easy or natural to do.
BRUCE COCKBURN

Gordie was Canada's first star, and because he was, he helped destroy the Canadian inferiority complex. After hearing him, you had a feeling like, "Hey, we're doing something, too." Gord's intonation was the key. There were so many folkies that I admired for their songwriting, but, often, they weren't in tune. Gord's intonation and his tempo was so crisp. He was my hero through the early years. I wanted to be him and it's why I do what I do, pure and simple. He's the reason we have so many songwriters. He brought a formal musicality to what he was doing, using vocal charts and arrangements; things you can't fake.
DAVID BRADSTREET

Years ago my husband and kids were in Toronto for a movie at Ontario Place, and it was Halloween. We took costumes and went through Rosedale. Gord was sitting out front with his guitar and handing out candy.
CHAR WESTBROOK

I proposed to my wife while 'The Wreck of the Edmund Fitzgerald' was on the radio. Seemed kind of symbolic of my single life.
DAVE REED

All of the conversations about Lightfoot, if they go on long enough, inevitably end in the same place, the little droppings littering his career, the embarrassments he has successfully kept from his fans by stage-managed interviews, circumspection, and maintenance of a strict, almost paranoid regimen of privacy.
TOM HOPKINS

I remember getting laid off from my job — a job that I really liked — and coming home and not wanting to think, feel, or do anything. I just wanted to be numb for awhile without worrying about whatever kind of shit lay ahead of me. I comatosed myself, and when I came out of it, I put on "Don Quixote," just because it was the last record that I'd pulled out, back when I had a job. Something about Gord's voice was assuring and positive. It had a courage and fearlessness to it because it wasn't your typical singing voice. It was singular and had personality. It was bold. It got me off the couch and made me get outside. If this guy could rise above whatever shit he'd had to deal with, then anyone could, I thought.
JAMES X

Gord, I was going to end this section with these stories but something just happened this weekend that I thought I should tell you about. Although I know we aren't really having a conversation or anything, it's what people who are having a conversation are supposed to do. Still, it's not like it's Monday morning in the coffee shop near the bus terminal and we run into each other and you ask, "So, how's that book of yours going, anyway?" and I tell you, "Oh, fine, although damned if

I can figure out what you were doing in August 1966." Then you say, "Hey, I'm keeping August 1966 for myself." I laugh, then you laugh, then we both laugh. Then you pat me on the shoulder and tell me that you're pretty sure that this is going to be the best book ever. I swoon, just a little. Then Ian Tyson walks in and shoots me with a crossbow.

These kinds of emotional swings are more or less what it feels like to be writing a book. There are good days and bad days. I'm sure you know the feeling, Gord. Sometimes the fog of thought clears and my mind is radiant, while, other times, I can't breathe. It's usually one or the other, although lately, it's been the other. Every writer who ever wrote anything feels at the back of his brain that all of the hours he's poured into his work will be for naught. No one will buy the book and no one will read it. Libraries will fling it into the dumpster, pristine and still fresh-smelling. Great and good people – nuns, firefighters, shelter workers, the Kielburger brothers – will appear on television stomping on the cover, declaring it an insolent and hateful work of pretentious garbage.

Then again: who knows. Maybe this book will find its readers. Maybe it will even win awards. As you can imagine, writers are desperate for readers and awards. Awards get you in the paper and they get you money. Awards lead to book sales which lead to positions in fancy universities teaching English or creative writing. But most writers don't get nominated, Gord. This is my tenth book and I have a few loyal readers, but I've never won any major awards. In fact, if you turn this book on its face, you'll see that it says: "Dave Bidini has yet to win any of Canada's major literary awards." I wanted to put that line in because it's funny, but I also wanted to prove a point. You see, because I write mostly about rock and roll and sports, I almost never get nominated for awards (although I won the F.G. Bressani Literary Prize for best Italian–Canadian writer in 2004. The award is blue and my son thinks it looks like a spaceship). Sometimes, it feels as if people in Canadian literature – not everyone, of course – couldn't give two shits about either of these subjects. And sometimes my books are funny, making me doubly screwed (there's an award for humour in Canada, but I've never been nominated for that, either). Judges and juries of big literary awards love books about death and tragedy and war and poverty and hardship, and even though my last book was about homelessness – it was not a funny book – that didn't do the trick. I have lots of friends who are writers and who read what I write, but most writers have never read my books, although Yann Martel has. Last year, I was invited to a literary conference where everyone sat around complaining about him. For some reason people seem jealous of his success. But I don't care. Yann Martel read one of my books and he sent it to Stephen Harper for him to read. I need to get him on one of those juries. Soon, I'd be winning awards, and models would be throwing themselves at me at parties in expensive downtown clubs. I'd be like Salman Rushdie at the Playboy Mansion or Henry Miller in Paris. Or maybe I'd just take Janet and the kids to Italy. It's probably what I'd do.

Gord, I hope I'm not boring you. But give me a moment longer to talk about writing and stuff (I'm getting to what happened this weekend, I promise). You see, as a published author, things have to happen other than winning awards to make writing worthwhile as a career, if not a vocation. These things don't have to be big or important. Sometimes, just seeing a pretty girl in smart glasses on the subway reading your book can be enough; or getting invited to a cool literary festival in a faraway part of Canada; or hearing someone interesting and famous mention one of your books during an interview; or having a film or TV producer tell you that he can see George Clooney playing you in the film adaptation of your book that will probably never get made; or being sent a cheque for four hundred dollars from Denmark for the rights to photocopy your book; or getting translated into Indonesian; or, in my case, being sent last weekend on an all-expenses-paid trip to Algonquin Park by a woman named Helen from Tourism Ontario, who organized a stay for me and my family at a lodge run by Voyageur Quest, an organization that does northern adventure tours. Of course, I told her, no way, I'm writing this book about Lightfoot and it's all very serious business and I have a seriously short deadline and all of that. But my wife said, you know, maybe not writing for a few days would be good. And because I couldn't breathe, I needed the break. The time away would be good and I'd never spent time in the park before. Besides, I read that you liked to take long canoe trips there, too – sometimes in an attempt to get clean; and sometimes to just get away – so I thought it might be an appropriate place to visit. I promised myself that I wouldn't write during my trip. Algonquin Park would be my literary detox. I'd arrive home feeling renewed.

We left Toronto on a late January morning in the thick of winter. As we rode the Ontario Northland express out of Union Station, we couldn't have been anywhere but on a Canadian train: the sound of its heavy chugging and plumes of steam filling the railyard; toqued passengers shuttling to their seats in down jackets pulling gym bags and stickerless suitcases behind them; seventies curtained windows revealing the yawning half-frozen lake then an old, nicotine-bearded man crossing a city bridge in a tattered Maple Leafs cap then smoke chimneying out of the stone-bricked Gooderham and Worts distillery then the forests of the Don Valley hanging heavy with new snow; and the northern destination cards on the back of the seats printed with the names of places like Washago, Hearst, New Liskeard, Smooth Rock Falls, and Temagami. Four hours later in South River – a town at the northwestern tip of the park – a nice young man named Mark picked us up and drove us in. Frost like elephant skin gathered on the windows of the van and the CBC played on the radio. The temperature hovered at minus 22, which was positively Floridian considering that, two days later, it would reach minus 41.

Our cabin was located at the edge of Round Lake, where a small rink had been scraped clean for skating. At night, it was painted by torchlight, and, on our first evening, we watched the orange moon rise from the far edge of the shoreline while

our kids played hockey using branches collected from the surrounding forests. The following day, we set out on skis across
the frozen lake into the woods, where we slid and scraped and
herringboned along trails carved into the knee-deep snow.
Occasionally, the young man, Mark, would stop, stare at the
ground, and show us animal tracks – moose, deer, coyote, and
wolf – and we'd listen to him speak before returning to nature's enormous silence. Before the trip, I'd always seen snow
as a force that works to hide the earth, but after being in the
deep woods, I saw how it reveals as much as it disguises, and
how busy the woods are even when quiet. We moved forward
on the trail looking for tracks, but it was often enough to float
across the land on Peltonen runners. My mind emptied itself
of this book, its music, and the life behind the words. It felt
good, Gord. Is this how you feel when you're here?

Eventually, we emerged from the woods into the cold
sunshine of a frozen lake. It was then that Mark stopped on
his skis and pointed to four or five long and jagged tracks
running deep over the snow in half-circles and diagonal lines
cutting towards the middle of the lake. They were fresh, he
said, having been made only a few hours earlier by wolves
hunting their prey, probably a deer, although he couldn't be
sure. We stood at the forest's stand and imagined what it
must have looked and sounded like, and how there were no
traces of the terrible and wild conflagration save for the paw
prints in the snow, which, after awhile, we skied towards,
studying the fine impressions, which, Mark told us, were
perfect because of the way wolves step into one another's

tracks in order to make as little sound as possible. This had all just happened. The animals had just been there. We sensed them watching us through secret eyes as we crossed the lake and headed home.

Later on in the cabin, Mark asked if we wanted to hear some music. We told him that it would be fine, so he pulled out a CD walkman and inserted a disc. The first song was John Prine doing something from *Jesus: The Missing Years*. I resisted telling Mark about my book. Then next song was early Dylan, and I laughed to myself, wondering, Gord, what you would have thought about this, being in Algonquin Park – your favourite spot, just a few hours away from where you grew up off Highway 11 – listening to these other singers who weren't you. Next came more Dylan. Then even more. Mark asked a question about the process of writing and I was about to tell him about the book when, all of a sudden, another song started. It was "Early Morning Rain." After that came "Sundown," then "Carefree Highway." And then came five or six more of your songs. When it ended, Mark put on a CD by a band called Caribou, who don't sound like you at all. Then again, they are named Caribou. I figure they probably never would have named themselves that had you not existed.

On Sunday, the coldest day of the year, we boarded the train home. Toronto was also in a deep freeze. Minus 18. The taxi driver home said you'd have to be either crazy – or a taxi driver, he joked – to be out in this weather.

It was a great trip, Gord. Coming home, I was ready to attack the book with renewed blood and revitalized spirit.

But then, the emails started coming one after another. The Facebook messages were also relentless. In the cafe where I sometimes write, a person asked me if I'd done what others had done on Sunday night: gone to Hugh's Room for the Gordon Lightfoot tribute. Of course, I hadn't. Because I was in the park, word of the tribute hadn't reached me, nor was I able to receive notices, one of which announced that you would be showing up yourself. You would play three songs at your own tribute, which would take place a few blocks away from where I lived, and, hold on a minute: who plays songs at their own tribute? Still, I felt crushed. No, I felt betrayed. What were you doing making such a broad public appearance when the person who is supposed to be telling the story of your life was away in a fucking cabin listening to the sound of the snapping fire and growling sled dogs and crackling ice thinking about anything but you even though you're all I've been thinking about for the past six months? Was this a trick or a joke? Were you and your gods in furry hats and lumberjack jackets trying to destroy me? After the show, people said, "I can't believe you weren't there; you know, writing a book about him and everything," and "Man, he was, like, talking to everyone," and "Wow, you know he's a really personable guy!" It was my chance and I missed it. Sunday turned into Monday. You still won't talk to me.

One thing saved me from not giving up on this book. It's not much, but it's all I've got. You see, last Friday was the one-year anniversary of my friend Paul Quarrington's death. I don't know if you know who he was, Gord, but he was the best writer ever and he was good to every young writer he ever met. While ruminating on these events, I thought that maybe, just maybe, he was behind all of this. Maybe he was messing with me (you and him both). Maybe he was telling me that it's things like this that make writers strong and turn good books into great books, the kind that win awards and get you sleeping with models, although, you know, Paul would have told me not to sleep with models unless I really have to because it hardly ever works out. I miss Paul because I miss not being able to tell him about things like this. Just hearing his voice would have relaxed me and filled me with confidence. One of the last bits of literary advice he ever gave me was: "Have you ever thought of writing a book about one person?" No, I told him, and I really hadn't thought about it before. Besides, I said, it would have to be the right person. It would have to be someone who would let me into his or her life. Otherwise, I'd have to force myself in. And I didn't think I had the strength for that. I can't remember what he said after that, but if he could hear me saying this now, I know what he'd tell me. He'd take a sip of his beer or whiskey, clear his throat once, scrape his chair closer to the table, and say, "Well, no one ever said it was supposed to feel good . . ." Of course, Paul is right. I guess I can't stop now.

Next chapter, Shakespeare.

'72

SATURDAY AND SUNDAY, JULY 15TH AND 16TH

O n Saturday and Sunday, the stars who weren't supposed to come to Mariposa came. Peter Goddard, writing in the *Toronto Star,* reported that: "Bob Dylan, rarely seen in the past five years, hugged Gordon Lightfoot before escaping from fans running after him. Neil Young led 4,000 in a singalong as Joni Mitchell looked on. Central to this was the slight figure of Dylan, who, in jeans, white shirt, and wearing a red bandana and rimless spectacles, wandered unrecognized with his wife, Sarah. He was given a bottle of beer by a passerby, then, circling, he stood briefly in a crowd watching some old fiddlers before moving to another area to listen to Roosevelt Sykes and Bukka White. 'We were vacationing in the area, and decided to drop in,' he said. 'We've been here for Mariposa's three days,' he said. 'We even got rained out like everyone else on Saturday night.'"

The day started like any other festival day. But then, according to Honey Novick, "stuff happened that just shouldn't

have happened." Apart from the Mariposa volunteers who'd
risen with the sun to catch the six and seven o'clock ferries,
those first to the grounds were the ones who'd squatted on
the island, sleeping on the north beach behind scrub weeds or
in a stand of trees in the thick of the park or beneath the
Gibraltar Point lighthouse, which loomed beside a canal perfect for bathing. The sun lurked behind a brew of grey clouds as
ticketholders scrambled aboard boats heading to the island,
where the sounds of Jean Ritchie singing ritual songs could
be heard from stage four. Over at the island marina, Tex
McLeod and his friends slept aboard a 1925 wooden sailboat,
which they'd sailed from Oakville. Leaving the suburbs on
Friday, they'd expected to find the marina jammed with those
who'd had the same idea, but when they pulled in that morning,
their craft was the only one docked for the purpose of going
to the festival. "There was a bunch of us on the boat," said Tex,
"and we had a great time. We went from this crazy festival
scene to the harbour, where we relaxed. It was perfect. I remember getting up on Saturday morning and walking around.
The day was moody and grey, but still great. I looked up the
road and approaching me was this tall and vivacious woman.
After a moment, I realized that it was Joni Mitchell."

Joni was the first musical interloper to the island, arriving with the smooth-faced and boyish Jackson Browne heeling
at her side, and Graham Nash of CSNY behind him. Ten
months earlier, the Saskatoon-born songwriter had released
her defining album, *Blue,* and, on June 15, 1972, she'd played
the last of her shows at the Olympia in Paris before returning

to California. Jackson Browne had opened much of the tour, and the two musicians had been linked romantically (Honey Novick remembered riding the ferry with them, and how "they couldn't keep their hands off each other"). *Blue* had eclipsed Mitchell's reputation as merely a folksinger – both artistically and commercially – and she'd become less the artist-at-the-end-of-the-block, and more of a serious pop icon. Unlike other strong female voices of the day such as Tina Turner or Bonnie Raitt or Joan Baez, who were linked to battle-ready sexual toughness or political relevance, Joni's power was entirely musical. Her new songs were finely composed and her voice – as well as her unusual and wide-toned acoustic guitar-playing – maintained its strength and richness even as it scaled octaves like a great bird swallowed by the sky. Unlike Neil Young – whose art was veering in a much darker, self-devouring direction – Joni's appearance at Mariposa symbolized positive musical and cultural change. If Canada was poised to shake itself free of its sixties patchouli fog, Joni was the hood ornament for a culture moving into the clearing of new times.

Storking along the banks of the canal, Joni must have looked to Tex like an ethereal figure: alabaster skin with high, sloping cheekbones and a striking overbite. She was tall, as well, with praying mantis arms and the legs of a colt, favouring finely-fabriced Topanga Canyon dresses that swept the ground. Her presence was an early sign that, over the next few days, things on Centre Island would be very different than planned.

Leigh Cline was Mariposa's technical director in 1972. It was his job to make sure that everything ran on schedule, and that all of the stages accommodated the festival's long list of performers. Remembering Saturday's events, Leigh said that "before any of the stars came, the festival was running smoothly, in as much as any festival can ever run smoothly. Things were still hectic, and below the surface, it was total madness, but there were no major screw-ups or incidents, even though we had a full crowd that weekend. In retrospect, I basically think that someone tapped me on the shoulder and said, 'They're here.' And it was our job to deal with all of that."

In 1972, organizers had added another wrinkle to the festival's layout: five or six small stages with music happening at the same time. "It was the first time anyone had tried it, but it's now the standard at most festivals," he said. "Because of this set up, we avoided big acts for whom the stages would have been too small. A sound company called Activated Air from Philadelphia brought in the system because nobody else in Canada had the kind of equipment to accommodate so many stages. We purposefully downsized things to make things more manageable. So, of course," he added, balefully, "this would be the year when the heavies decided to show up."

Cline suggested that, in order to understand the effect that the guests had on the crowd, you had to consider where Canadian music was on its evolutionary scale. He said, "Because the whole folk scene was dying down, having people like Joni around on Saturday meant causing a new kind of impact that people hadn't really felt before. But the weekend's 'surprise' performances also had the potential to pull people from the other stages. We had a lot of traditional performers

Bernie Fiedler and Murray McLauchlan at Mariposa, 1972

who weren't used to playing to huge, urban audiences, period, and because they were [already] out of their element, it would have made matters even worse if whatever crowd was there all of a sudden stood up and left. Because of this, some people felt that the guests absolutely should not play. Others said, 'Sure, they should play; they're our friends. Just because Joni has become successful doesn't mean that she can't come back home.' Others threw up their hands and said that they didn't know what to do. There were discussions in the trailer. Graham Nash told us that he absolutely would not play. He was a real gentleman. A real nice guy."

After a series of meetings, Cline and his fellow organizers thought they'd come up with a way of accommodating the guests. "During the Monday night Hootenannies at the Riverboat – and in most coffee houses at the time – it was an unspoken rule that if the main performer invited a guest up to play, the limit was three songs. The deal worked out between the festival and Murray McLauchlan and Bruce Cockburn's manager, Bernie Finkelstein, was similar," and it also adhered to the Toronto Musician's Association's standards, which the festival was required to observe. McLauchlan – who had been linked romantically to Ms. Mitchell – consented without hesitation, halving his set to service an appearance by his old friend. Remembering Joni's set – she played five songs on dulcimer and guitar – Colin Linden said that "she performed a new song, 'You Turn Me On, I'm a Radio,' which we all know now as a famous tune, a great tune. But back then, it was totally new. It was the first time she'd ever played it live." Gordon Klager remembers that, when he got to the festival on Saturday, "you could just feel that something was going to happen. Before Murray McLauchlan's set, I remember someone in the crowd saying, 'Hey, I think that's Joni Mitchell,' and when we looked over, I saw this head pop up near the artist's tent at the side of the stage and then disappear. After Murray introduced her, the crowd went wild. She came out looking so ethereal. So young. She'd just come out with *Blue*, so those songs sounded very fresh, very real. It was magical watching her."

Ken Whiteley said, "Joni was just Joni; she'd been there before. I saw her at Innes Lake at the '64 festival, wearing a long evening gown and long golden hair. She was quite upset after her set because there had been a bunch of yahoos yelling

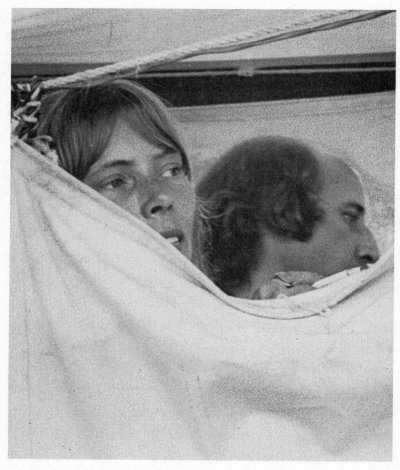

Joni Mitchell with Bernie Fiedler

at her while she was playing. A few months later, she came down to the Riverboat on a Monday night Hootenanny, and she was transformed. There was a folk radio program out of Boston and I remember hearing that Tom Rush was going to cover 'Urge to Go.' The next time I saw her, she was in a miniskirt, with short hair, doing all of her own songs. Because Mariposa and the Toronto folk scene had deep history with her, it wasn't unexpected when she turned up. And, frankly, because so many of the festival-goers were into blues and swing and French and Newfoundland music, her surprise perform-ance didn't create the kind of impact that would have hap-pened had Dylan been allowed to play."

For a moment, organizers worried that Joni's appear-ance would prove too much for the small festival to handle because, according to Cline, "the backstage area was separ-ated only by a red snow fence, and all we had on site was folkie security." Still, there were no major incidents. Joni and Jackson – and their shows – coexisted easily with everything else that was going on, and, as the crowd and volunteers sailed across the harbour at nightfall on Saturday, organizers gathered at the Executive Motor Hotel at King Street and Bathurst to wipe their brows, feeling grateful that they'd avoided any trouble.

One of the people riding the boat that evening was a young volunteer, Kathleen Miller, who, along with a handful of others, disembarked at Front Street before walking up half a dozen blocks to Dundas, over to Yonge, and then north to Carlton, where Stones fans had jammed the thoroughfare outside Maple Leaf Gardens, swallowing lost streetcars and painting the scene in total denim. "It was a trippy weekend for me," said Miller, "because I took [Bonnie Raitt's bassist] Freebo to see the Stones at the Gardens. He had a degree in law and he was soft spoken. He was also great in bed, so, you know, we hung out." Inside the arena, the Stones crowd was — like the Stones themselves — ragged and bloodshot, ripped on eighteen kinds of pharmaceuticals and great plugs of black and red hash sealed in foil and stamped with a gold insignia. People huffed joints as fat as corn cobs and slugged from wine-skins as they watched the tour's opening act, Stevie Wonder — in long robes and cornrows — rock back and forth on his keyboard bench while grinning, face twisted, into the rafters of the legendary building. At the end of Stevie's set, the lights went up. The crowd had the damaged look of victims after an earthquake. If the wicker-basketed denizens of Mariposa had planned for sustenance and stayed hydrated, the Gardens crowd sat blottoed in their seats picking from whatever was left in their plastic bags. If Mariposa had been policed by portly men in windbreakers and elephant pants, the Gardens was crawling with cops who arrested twenty people and booted out another hundred and the air was thick and hot and gluey and when the Stones came on Keith looked out into the crowd and saw worms with hands and hair wriggling to a beat that he fought to stay with so Charlie slammed the snare hard harder hardest to help his wavering bandmates steady them-selves and just get through this goddamned show before going to Montreal which everyone did except Keith who drugged himself to sleep in his hotel in Toronto but shit it was Friday or was it Tuesday and where was I and who am I and fuck Dylan and everybody else but the beast rolled on and got big bigger biggest and if Mariposa was the last gasp of hippie idyll then the Stones at the Gardens showed that whatever had come together could be undone because it was heaven and hell, past and future all in one city. All in one night.

Back at the Executive, Cline remembers thinking, "Well, we made it through. It's over. It wasn't a disaster." But then all of sudden the air escaped from the room. Someone walked in and said, "Well, guys, I just talked to [publicist] Richard Flohil. Bob Dylan's in town and he's coming to the island tomorrow."

Before Mariposa, Dylan hadn't been in hiding, but he hadn't been out much, either. In June of that year, he'd gone to see Elvis Presley play at Madison Square Garden (John Lennon, George Harrison, David Bowie, and Art Garfunkel were there, too), but other than that, his visibility and creative output were limited. His last album, *Self Portrait,* had been released in 1970, and, in 1972, his only work was writing the soundtrack to and acting in the Sam Peckinpah film, *Pat Garrett and Billy the Kid* (*More Greatest Hits,* a collection, was also released that year). In August 1969 he played the Isle of Wight festival and in 1971 he played the Concert for Bangladesh. But he wouldn't tour again until 1974. Had he played Mariposa, it would have been the kind of musical event remembered and noted for generations. Instead, the festival would end up denying the greatest songwriter of his generation a chance to take the stage.

No one can confirm whether or not Dylan was there on Saturday, even though Goddard quotes him as saying that he was. Fifteen-year-old Bradley Hardy is certain that he saw him during Joni Mitchell's early evening mini-set. He remembers noticing Dylan standing "beyond a snow fence with a white styrofoam cup in his hand talking to people. We got our cameras out and I'm pretty sure that he was aware of us. At the time I had a Russian-built 35mm camera which took fabulous pictures, but it was as manual as a camera could be. It had a special ring on the lens that you had to shut down after you focused, an irritating extra step that I often forgot to take. Joni Mitchell was playing at the main stage and everyone was sitting watching. I was at the back of the crowd and Joni was so far away that she was about an eighth of an inch in height, but there was a well-defined path leading towards the stage. I moved forward along the path until it collapsed into the crowd, leaving me well back from the stage front and out of photo range. At this point I turned around and looked back. This guy was walking towards me along the same path. It was Bob Dylan and it was amazing; just me and Bob Dylan. I was instantly aware of the potential. I was overwhelmed, stunned, filled with adrenaline. I levelled the camera at him and focused, but he kept walking towards me. All he had to do was pause for a split second, but he didn't. I took a couple of photos as he brushed by me and walked towards the stage. I don't know what happened after that. I don't think he ever made it to the stage."

Musician Michael Laderoute agrees with Bradley that Dylan was there on Saturday. He said that he was watching the New Lost City Ramblers play at a small stage, sipping beer at a picnic table. He remembers: "I gave one to some other fellow sitting at the same table. There was an interview published later with Dylan that quoted him as saying that he'd watched the Ramblers while having a beer at a picnic table. To this day I think I had a beer with Bob Dylan." David Bradstreet, the songwriter and 1977 Juno Most Promising Artist winner who also played at the '72 fest, ran into Dylan on Saturday night at the Executive Motor Hotel. He recalls walking into a room with his guitar and sitting down with a group of people bashing away on guitars, one of whom was Bonnie Raitt. Then Bob Dylan showed up. "He stood next to me, and I remember thinking, 'Oh, that's what weak in the knees feels like.' I was nineteen years old and it was amazing for me, just being in the presence of someone like him, someone who'd had such an enormous impact on what we all did back then and what we all still do. Someone told me that he was there to see Leon Redbone, but I'm not sure if that's true. It would have made sense because they had an affinity for each other's music, or at least Dylan did for Leon. Leon had an air of mystery about him, and after Dylan's motorcycle accident, some people thought he was Bob in disguise. When Leon lived in Toronto, he was a mysterious figure. When anyone asked if they could contact him, he gave out the number of a pool hall at the corner of Yonge and Bloor. You were supposed to ask for 'Grunt,' and then somebody would go and get him. I really liked him. He was an interesting guy and a great musician."

Kathleen Miller — who was also a volunteer responsible for looking after Taj Mahal and his brother — came over on a boat with Dylan on Sunday morning. "Taj, his brother, and I got on the little ferry with maybe twenty people sitting near the front on the left," she said, "and just as it was pulling out,

Taj Mahal at Mariposa, 1972

this short guy jumped on and started looking for somewhere to sit. I moved over. Taj leaned over to him and asked, 'Hey man, how's it going? Are you gonna play?' I took a closer look and realized it was Dylan. Earlier in the day, the airwaves were filled with announcements that he was going to play and, as a result, the island was complete havoc on Sunday. It has certainly been a story I've told over the years. Bob Dylan sat down beside me."

Lightfoot arrived on the island around the same time as Dylan, although he kept his presence well hidden. It's possible that he stayed mostly in the artist tents, although few of the area coordinators remember him hanging out backstage. Maybe he lurked in the woods, smoking and peering out. Or maybe he waited on the mainland until the last minute before ferrying across, where he sought out the Good Brothers' hippiefolk klatch, who knew that the best way to comfort the insecure legend was to pass him a guitar.

On Sunday, Lightfoot and Dylan eventually found each other, but both managed to circulate for a time without being discovered. David Bradstreet confirmed that "from what I know, Dylan had been on the island for a lot of the day, and with the exception of some sort of clamour near the end, people were respectful of his space. In general, I think that Canadians are cool about this stuff. If there's a celebrity walking around in New York, for instance, people will shout after them, they'll call attention. But here, it's more of a 'just don't look' kind of mentality. We're not that demonstrative compared to other people. I had a nice conversation with Joni

Mitchell that weekend, too. She was who she was, but she was also just this nice person, without any airs or pretension. Still, if people weren't yelling 'Hey, it's Bob Dylan!' it was certainly on everybody's lips. People resisted getting carried away, and he must have appreciated that."

There were other forces at play that managed to insulate the songwriter from getting besieged by fans, at least in the beginning. Because the idea of one of the world's most popular musicians attending a small island festival was, in its essence, preposterous, most festival-goers *pfffted* as rumours started to spread. In 1972, legions of folksingers looked like Dylan, anyway, and in most cases, if someone had spotted him buying beads or in the lineup for the falafel truck, it was more than likely a doppleganger or Zimmerman wannabe. Not only that, but one's perception of reality wouldn't have been exact considering the climate of the times. Someone's friend might have thought they'd seen him, but they'd probably seen Sirhan Sirhan, Lord Byron, and Scooby-Doo, too. It might not have been part of Dylan's grand design, but a crowd affected by hallucinogens wouldn't have been the worst setting in which a famous person might choose to wander.

Jean Francis, the northern hostel operator, recalls: "My memory is fuzzy, but I'm certain that I saw Bob Dylan early on Sunday afternoon. I was walking around the island by myself when I noticed this person hanging out near the trees in an empty part of the park. He was totally alone and, after a moment, I realized it was Dylan. He was playing harmonica by himself in the bushes. It was a very intimate moment, very personal. But then a few more people came over, wondering what I was looking at. I guess he must have noticed, because he stopped. To this day, I'm not really sure this happened, but something in my memory tells me that it did. Afterwards, we lay out on the grass and crashed from the MDA. I don't remember much else and I was completely unaware of the riot that happened later. It's not like we had computers or BlackBerries or anything, and that's why Bob was probably able to just go off and do what he wanted to do. Something could have been happening in one part of the island and the other part would have had no idea what was going on."

When Cline first heard the news, he tried to get confirmation. Richard Flohil said that he hadn't actually seen Dylan, but that he was told he was coming. Then, according to Cline, "After making a few calls, he came back and said, 'We have a problem.'" Although Neil and Joni and Lightfoot were idolized by legions of fans, Cline said that "Dylan was ten levels above them; there was always a mystique about him from day one." Because of this, organizers were presented with a unique situation: having to decide whether or not the greatest songwriter of their generation should be allowed to impact on the wellness and stability of the festival as it played out that weekend on the small island at the bottom of the city.

The Dylanmania that ended up consuming the festival started as a slow boil. One of the people responsible for making sure that it did not affect the day's proceedings was area manager coordinator Marna Snitman, who, on Saturday, dropped Valium for the first (and last) time in order to smooth her fraying nerves. Because of the stars' presence, her fellow festival lieutenants met every five minutes to determine what to do with all of the surprise performers. "In past festivals, I could just put away my board member hat and concentrate on helping the area managers. But that weekend, it was one thing or another, with a lot of very serious decisions having to be made. Nineteen seventy-two was a real turning point. It was a test of Estelle Klein's philosophy, which was, basically, a 'no star' philosophy. Because the Stones were in town, rumours actually started on Friday that Mick Jagger was going come, so, subconsciously, I think we were primed for what happened." Echoing Cline's words, Snitman said that "because Joni (and also Neil) had long been associated with the scene, it wasn't too weird. I wasn't surprised. What did surprise me, however, was the groundswell among the other performers – a kind of wariness – who cautioned the board to not let the stars steal audiences from other stages. It was hard to prevent. I was standing at the back of the audience at one workshop when all of a sudden a buzz started that one surprise performer or another had shown up, and the audience emptied. I was devastated for the performers. I remember someone – I think it was Owen McBride – being quite upset. You couldn't blame them, but the board was getting raked over the coals." Reminded of the pervasive anti-star sentiment, Bruce Cockburn said, "If certain members of the folk community thought that the star shit shouldn't be happening, I didn't care. It was certainly attached to my notion of how things were supposed to be, but I wasn't like the other folkies, one of whom once told me that they would never make a record because 'it freezes you where you are.' Besides, the angst and resentment expressed by this faction didn't translate to the audience. From what I gathered, they loved it that the guests showed up. They could appreciate all that was unfolding that day, and, really, if you were a music fan, who wouldn't have?"

While this may have been the case for the great part of the crowd, a July 27 letter to the *Toronto Star* expressed another sentiment entirely. The author of the letter wrote: "There was an incident on Sunday [at the Mariposa Folk Festival] which disturbed us. We were listening to a concert by Owen McBride, when, suddenly, a large part of the audience tore over to the next area to watch Neil Young. This was a very embarrassing experience for the people watching McBride's concert."

Snitman said that "there was a lot of bitterness, a lot of anger, but I don't see how we could have done it any differently. Joni had played for her first big crowds ever at Mariposa. Neil had written 'Sugar Mountain' after singing with Vickie Taylor at the Riverboat. These musicians' roots were genuine. I think it would have been wrong for us not to let them play." What Marna doesn't mention is that, as soon as McLauchlan – and, later, Bruce Cockburn – decided to give up half of their scheduled stage time to Joni and Neil, the complaints from other artists lessened as they realized that someone other than themselves would provide for the guests. In the end, it was cold comfort that, even if they were abandoned by the crowds, at least their stage time was uncompromised.

Marna said that "it was a very tough decision when Dylan showed up. There were lots of mixed feelings. We huddled and tried to decide what to do. Finally, the decision – which fell to festival president Buzz Chertkoff in Estelle's absence – was to not let Dylan play. I think it was fine, either way, with him. He looked as good as he's ever looked: red bandana, white shirt, and blue jeans. He hadn't been seen in public for awhile, so it was a kind of confirmation that he was still around, still happening. He wandered around with his wife and son, Jesse, and, for us, it was a source of pride that he could just hang out without being hounded. Sure, you dream about what it would have been like to hear him, but in the end, the festival wasn't any lesser because of this. When he finally left the island with Leon Redbone, we'd dodged a bullet. We were patting ourselves on the back, shouting: 'We did it, we did it!' It was a great moment."

But, for Snitman and the others, the situation was only starting to get complicated. As they watched Dylan and his friend float away, something astonishing happened: the water taxi turned around. Snitman recalls: "We saw him cross the harbour, but then the boat turned around. We thought: 'What the fuck is going on here?' The guy was coming back. By then, everyone knew he'd been there and the crowds started to gather. That's when it became a problem."

No one knows what Bob and Leon talked about during their aborted trip to the mainland, but, if subsequent events are any indication, it's likely that Redbone, the mixer, talked Dylan into returning with the intent to take the stage. Now, the superstar who'd been happy to simply hang out and enjoy the festival was back with renewed purpose.

Ken Whiteley found himself backstage at the moment that Dylan asked if he could perform. Whiteley – one of Canadian music's longstanding Balthasars – was playing Mariposa for the first time with his group, The Original Sloth Band, which also featured his older brother, Chris. They'd been part of the event before – both Ken and Chris had played the new songwriter's workshop in 1969 – but the 1972 festival, he said, "was the beginning of the rest of my life. It was my confirmation. It wasn't until after our set at Mariposa that I really knew what I wanted to do."

Ken had first gone to Mariposa in 1964 in Toronto. "The festival moved to Maple Leaf Stadium after the town fathers from Orillia got together and decided to ban it. I was thrilled that it was all happening in Toronto. There was no way my parents were going to a let a thirteen-year-old go to Orillia, but since we went to [the AAA International League's Toronto] Maple Leaf games all the time at the stadium, they let me go to this one. I remember Lightfoot opening the Friday night set. Someone introduced him as 'Orillia's own . . .' but he was cannon fodder as people were walking in. Obviously, things had changed for him in 1972. He wasn't just that guy from Orillia anymore.

"Other than all of these great musicians being together – Taj Mahal, Bonnie Raitt, John Prine, et cetera – '72 didn't really feel like anything out of the ordinary until Dylan showed up wanting to play. It was close to happening. I saw it backstage with my own eyes. Michael Cooney, the host, was telling Bob that under no circumstances could he appear. You could tell that Bob wanted to, but the organizers had made a decision. Cooney said, 'Bob, I don't think it's fair to everybody else to let you play. If you play, everyone will leave the other stages.'"

Cooney confirmed Ken's recollection: "Because I'd met Dylan before, at the 1963 Berkeley Folk Festival, there was a point of reference between us, and I was given the task of having to talk him into not playing. Dylan wore a red bandana, and we could spot him easily sitting in the crowd, even though he wasn't recognized by others. I hosted two workshops – 'Music of the twenties, thirties, and forties,' and 'Songs so bad, they're good,' featuring Leon Redbone – and Dylan came to both. I had talked Estelle into hiring Leon – she didn't really like him – and, a few months after the festival, Dylan mentioned how much he liked him in an interview with *Rolling Stone*. That's how Leon got his record deal, and he's thanked me for booking him ever since."

Cooney explained to Dylan that, while Joni Mitchell's appearance had gone well the day before, he was worried that Dylan playing would affect the festival. After he said this, Dylan just "sort of stood there and didn't say anything." Cooney remembered that "there was a weird teenager with him who did all of the talking. The kid kept saying, 'but, but, but . . .' as a way of replying for Bob. It was very strange. I have no idea who this kid was." While most people remembered the bulk of Dylan's entourage – his son, Jesse, wife,

Sarah, musician David Bromberg, and friend, The Paupers'
Adam Mitchell — no one else remembered Cooney's "weird
kid." Knowing what we know about the fantastic nature of the
event, and the events of that week, it's as if Cooney's "weird
kid" was conjured out of the day's circumstances, a figure
born from a Dylan lyric.

Whiteley ended up performing at the "Music of the twenties, thirties, and forties" workshop. After seeing what had
gone down with Bob and Michael (Whiteley has no recollection of Cooney's weird kid, either), the now-venerated blues-
man remembers: "When we looked out during our set, there
was Bob Dylan, watching us. I think we stumbled through the
first few minutes of our song before we could pull it together.
I remember seeing my one-year-old niece, Jenny, sitting near
Bob. She rolled a ball to him; Dylan picked it up and rolled
it back. They did that for most of the set. Later on, Gordon
Lightfoot came out of nowhere and sat with them. They were
in the audience, and I was on stage. I'd been a musician for a
long time, but coming home from the ferry on the last night of
the festival, I knew that something had changed. Suddenly, it
was all very clear to me."

People have long debated whether or not things would
have played out differently had Estelle Klein been on site
during the festival. Marna Snitman recalls: "Estelle Klein was
very strong, very bright, and very hardcore in her beliefs as
they related to festivals and folk music. She was the goddess of
folk festivals. She was brilliant, soft-spoken, but you never
crossed her. She was an extraordinary person, but there were

times when it became too much. I did what I did for the festival because we loved it and we loved her vision. She was generous to a fault. Because of these things, Buzz — the acting director and president — wanted to be very proper and careful when it came to major decisions regarding the surprise guests. He made sure that everyone on the board agreed with the decision. The undercurrent, of course, was that everybody was afraid of what Estelle would say when she got back, and that's probably why we deliberated so much. When she returned from Greece, we asked her what she thought, and she said: 'I would have done it differently.' It was hard to hear. But it wasn't entirely unexpected."

In an email from China, where he now teaches, Buzz wrote that "I was festival president, and the buck stopped with me. There was a difference in the decisions I had to make with Joni and Neil, because there was much greater pressure with respect to Dylan. It was made clear to me that had I permitted Dylan to go on stage, our most relied-upon local artists would never play Mariposa again. They felt that they would lose their audiences from all the other stages if Dylan performed." He wrote, "It was up to me to tell Dylan (through Adam Mitchell) that although he was most welcome to enjoy our festival, he would not be allowed to perform at it." Chertkoff's narrative contradicts Cooney's story, although it's possible that the president — whose presence was required all over the island that day — might not have known that Dylan had returned to the island in hopes of performing. Whatever the case, Chertkoff admitted that denying Dylan the chance to play was a decision that haunted him for years, especially since Estelle Klein later said that she would have placed him in a singer-songwriter workshop. Buzz still struggles with his call. He wrote that "the controversy raised by my decision is what prompted me to quit Mariposa for years."

After Dylan's return, the tenor of the festival changed, and it wasn't long before he had to be spirited away from the island for good. Michael Laderoute said that "after people discovered that he was there, there was all kinds of commotion. People were rowing boats across from the mainland trying to get to Centre Island, and some people were swimming across, too. It was pretty insane. There was this red snow-fencing around the perimeter, and I remember people trying to get to Dylan, who was being taken backstage. Security was trying to hold them back, but the fence was bending. It held, but you wonder what would have happened if it had snapped."

Dylan was spotted leaving a workshop, and the crowd converged upon the famous songwriter. He was pursued by fans who left their blankets and rucksacks behind them, and because it was Sunday, revellers getting their last licks for the weekend would have drawn extra courage after draining their wineskins and emptying their pipes. It must have been quite a sight: hundreds of raggedy folksingers trying to catch their hero. Dylan and his family moved along with a chevron of festival personnel, who brought him a second time to the boat, which ferried him to the mainland. One of the people who chased him was musician and publisher Pete Otis, who remembers: "It was like Jesus Christ himself was among us, and this was our opportunity to get close. We were all so excited that he was in our midst. Even after he was out of sight, my friend turned to me and said, 'Man, I don't know why I'm running. But I have to keep running.' Then, he just disappeared. It was symbolic in a way, because at the end of that day, everything just seemed a little different." In the end, maybe what Pete and the rest of the crowd were chasing was more than just a guy in a red bandana and cotton shirt. Maybe they were chasing themselves, their youth, and the last vestige of their disappearing times.

Tex McLeod left just after Dylan left. His friends returned the boat to its Oakville marina, and as he was being dropped off that evening on the 401 waiting to hitchhike home, a guy stopped to pick him up. When he looked in the window, he saw that it was Stan Rogers, the great singer. Stan drove him to 115 and they talked about how amazing it was to be part of such a great festival. While they drove, the radio was on and the broadcaster – who had a low, flat tone and slight nasal squeak – described how the RCMP had captured three more Millhaven inmates, which left only four at large. By the end of the summer, most of the others would be captured, including Donald Oag, who was found a few miles from the prison after attempting to return there from Ottawa, suggesting he wanted to be let back inside. The only remaining fugitive would be Streto Dzambas, who had confounded police for four months until, in early November, the OPP received a tip from INTERPOL that a man fitting Dzambas' description had been arrested in rural Yugoslavia for nearly killing his father. Dzambas spent his remaining time in a Balkan prison. The men who had sprung free that Tuesday evening in July were now contained. The ghosts had been pushed back into their box.

LETTER IN WHICH I TALK ABOUT WHAT I'M NOT SUPPOSED TO TALK ABOUT

Songs. They kept coming for you, Gord. Great songs, too: "Steel Rail Blues," "Pride of Man," and two Hall of Famers: "The Way I Feel" and "Early Morning Rain." Maybe it's hyperbolic to suggest that those last two compositions were the saddest and most moving works of their era, but why the fuck not. Babes have flown. Something is lost. The guitar-playing vagrant watches as his loves fucks off, and he is helpless to follow. In the lyrics – and in your persona, really – you create a place where tough and sad meet, where the strong man is weakened by the world's forces. Guys dig it because every guy has this place that he is programmed not to reveal – a sad and tender place, a feminine sensitivity in all of us; well maybe not in people who play thrashcore – and women like it because of your fearlessness when it comes to revealing that side. Gale Zoe Garnett suggested: "It's about a train or a car or a boat, so guys can understand and feel the music without admitting that they're moved by pure matters of the heart." The dockworker or grape-picker or carpenter bawls his eyes out because, man, he's singing about a train. But you're not. We know you're not. Still, you make it easy for us. You wrote these songs at the height of peace and love and freedom. What you're saying is that these things have their price, and that price is exacted from the walls of one's heart, the pulp of one's skin. No one else was writing like this. You told us, you told the world, that even though things were swerving upwards, sadness and pain was okay, too. Because if you believe that everything was sunshine and peppermints in the sixties, then you've been watching too many *Trouble with Tracy* reruns. The sixties ideology never really hit the countryside the way it did the big cities, anyway. You came from the country. You provided the grace of understanding. And that's why we don't cringe when we hear "Early Morning Rain" the way we do when we hear "California Dreamin'" or "Are You Going to San Francisco?" Fuck San Francisco. This is Canada. Things are cold and empty and sad here.

With your first record, and then your next (*The Way I Feel*, the title song re-recorded with an electric ensemble), you toured you ass off. You played everywhere, and you were making huge coin. You were played every few minutes on the radio, in Canada and in the U.S.A. You were an eight-year overnight success doing what you'd always wanted to do. The town of Orillia proclaimed August 5, 1967, "Gordon Lightfoot Day." And then came "The Canadian Railroad Trilogy."

I'm pausing for a moment because the nature of this song, commissioned by the CBC for the centennial year, demands a few paragraphs of consideration. It's the first song written that ever matched the size and breadth of Canada. I know it's hard to describe a song for those who haven't heard it, but I doubt that many people have not. Collins writes, "In 1967, it was impossible to turn on the radio without hearing it," even though it was never officially released as a single. The concept in itself boggles the mind: radio station music directors used to programming three-minute singles carving out time to accommodate a seven-minute epic about the birth of the CPR. I imagine the country's listeners stopping whatever they were doing to allow themselves a long moment to rise and fall and rise along with the song's dynamic, carried through the pulses and the rests, the hammer swings and the trundling locomotives that propel the tune. Whether you heard it in St. John's or Port Alberni, Calgary or Point Anne, Resolute Bay or Val D'Or, the listener's life as a Canadian was sewn into the storytelling. There's a popular tradition in music commissioned for national events that, usually, expresses patriotic fervour mixed with a celebratory and self-congratulatory glow. Very few of them talk about the fate of migrant navvies, or the blood, sweat, and devotion necessary to build the land into what it is today. "Canadian Railroad Trilogy" is the musical equivalent of a novel by Guy Vanderhaeghe, or maybe it's the other way around. In any case, on the heels of its release, anyone who'd ever picked up a guitar and tried to write a song was left terrified. First came your perfectly economical and true songs of love and pain. Then, a seven-minute panorama of a country.

Oh, man.

In '66, '67, '68, it was all great, so great. But I wouldn't be writing this book if these events weren't shadowed by something darker. Like writer Tom Hopkins once said in an article from 1978: "To talk of Lightfoot, you must talk of tragedy." A friend of mine put it another way: "What defines us as we age is how we deal with not being at thirty where we thought we'd be at eighteen." I'd add a caveat to that: what defines some of us is how we deal with being at thirty exactly where we thought we'd be at eighteen. I suppose that's an obtuse way of saying, that, through all of this — through the Carnegie Hall shows and Johnny Carson appearances and your exultant return to Massey Hall, to say nothing of Mariposa appearances that happened after you and Whelan were initially rejected by festival programmers — there were complications and sacrifices. The first thing to be sacrificed was your marriage, which never fell in step with your pursuit to fulfill your creative desires. Desires. Now, there's a word.

Okay, Gord, here comes the heavy shit. But first: a story. I found it on the Internet. It's a pretty funny excerpt. I'm putting it here because what follows a few paragraphs down isn't really very funny (I'm plying you with humour here, Gord). Anyhow, here it is:

"Interviewer: So what have you got next in the way of records? How many times have you been asked that question?

(Lightfoot turns slightly and farts loudly into the microphone)."

Okay, Gord: the heavy shit. I've heard lots of stories, and who knows how many of them are true. I'm sure that some of them are total bullshit, and I'm sure that some of them are not. I dunno. Someone told me once that one of the reasons why you didn't want to talk to me – or any other writer like me – is because we'd ask you about the drinking and the drugs and the married life and being with Cathy Evelyn, although she did a pretty good job of addressing that stuff in her own book, which, again, might have been made up of lies, or truths, or something in between (and which you should not read), though I don't know for sure. When I called your record company asking for interviews, I told them this: that here was a chance for you to set the record straight, to leave a proper story behind about all of the things that people say and think about you, rightly or wrongly. That message probably never got to you, which is why I'm telling you this here, even though it's obviously too late. I hope I get stuff right, but it's hard without knowing for sure. I don't want to slather more half-truths or untruths over you, but being a musician myself, maybe I can put it in context. There's nothing worse than some dweeb-ass music writer who's never swung a guitar thinking they know the life, so, maybe, Gord, you can count this book as a blessing. Still, I hope that what I'm about to write doesn't hurt you because, really, all I'm doing is trying to understand without tearing down something that, honestly, I relate to and respect in the highest order.

Okay: the boozing. It happens. I know this first hand. All artists do, but mostly musicians. After all, what other job do you show up for where someone – usually a very pretty girl with shiny hair wearing some cool band T-shirt moving with a low slope and eyes traced in blue charcoal – brings a tray of cold beers to your dressing room, with a bottle of whiskey on the side, maybe a snort of coke or pot bag if your manager has phoned ahead and asked politely in cellphone whispers. Whatever you want, you can get, even in the dives, because if bar owners don't have money, at least they have booze. The beers go down fine and the life is easy to get used to. Four beers and one joint. That used to be my friend's way of relaxing on stage and playing his best. But we drink for other reasons, too. We drink because of doubts and a fleeting sense of self-worth and the family shit and the fickle curve of success and crowds and attention, which dip and swing like an amusement park ride. Shit, even when things are good, that's even more reason to crack a few, to stay out too late, to party, and, if the pretty girl stays for your set and buys your record and says that she digs your stuff, well, maybe you go home with her for more drinks, although it usually doesn't get to that. Usually, she grabs you or you grab her and before you know it it's morning and the bass player has tracked you down and is pounding on the door trying to wake you up. On the next bus ride to wherever, you sleep in the back seat or, if you're lucky, the bunk bed or banquette of a tour bus listening to the idle chatter of your bandmates, whose conversation, inevitably, is about you and how it's been four weeks of this behaviour already, and should they be worried? Mostly, they decide that they should not be worried and they keep going. Gotta stay with the gig. Gotta pay the bills. Besides, if the rooms are big and soft and the songs easy, they look past the trouble no matter how bad it is. You threaten them whenever someone has the courage to confront you – you take a swing, maybe land a punch – and even after that, your band looks beyond it. Sometimes they swing back, but by then, their fate has been sealed. Fuck them. You'll do whatever the fuck you want to do and damned if some shit-ass jobbing drummer is going to tell you otherwise.

I have a friend, also a musician. We were kids when we first met, and playing rock and roll was the best. More and more people started coming to his shows because the music was getting better. Other bands would have to kick him out of rehearsal spaces to get him to leave. We were both writing hundreds of songs, playing four-hour shows. We were in command of our instruments, and because we were, we could express whatever musical ideas came our way. We felt strong, and we were young. Long hours and endless bus rides meant nothing to us. We all lived from gig to gig and even though the hours and the pressure and the lifestyle affected us, it didn't matter. We believed in rock and roll and our belief paid off. We knew that it couldn't last forever, of course, but that only made us play with greater intensity, thinking that any gig could be the last.

One night, after my friend had been especially bad, I poured him out of the car and into his apartment. Before he got out, I said to him, "I'm just wondering what the fourteen-year-old you would say to the twenty-three-year-old you?" He gave me a glassy, drunken stare that softened after he measured the weight of my words, and then he said, slouching back in the passenger seat, "You think there's something wrong with me?" I told him, "No, no. There's nothing wrong with you," because there wasn't, not yet. It was just drinking and I thought that, like anyone, he could stop if I held up a mirror to him. I told him, "It's just that you've been drinking a lot lately." He looked at me and waved his arm, "Awww, *pffft,*" he said. "It's okay." Then he grew kind of sad. "You think I need help or something?" I told him, "I dunno, yeah, maybe. But maybe you should just stop." He looked at me. No, he looked through me. Then he said, "Well, thanks, eh?" I told him no problem. Then he left the car, staggering into his flat.

The moment seems so innocent considering what would follow over the next few years: sleeping with women just so he could stay in their nice apartments; spending all of his money on booze; showing up later and later for his band's rehearsals; getting aggressive at times, and generally souring on people and the world; nearly burning to death in a couple of apartment fires; appearing with a bandaged this or broken that after drunken mishaps; and fostering a lifestyle that limited our contact: if you wanted to see him, you either had to go to his local bar to socialize or go to his apartment to work. Worse, when he did work, the work was great and the times really fun. But then the work, and the good times, hit a wall. He became a sour drunk after his seventh or eighth beer. He'd grouse about a life that was supposed to be free and beautiful, but had grown into something else. After awhile, I'd had enough. I was tired and sad. My friend got evicted, at which point I and a few others decided to do something about it. We staged a quasi-intervention, but, looking back, it was probably too little, too late. The intervention was a failure; we had no idea what we were doing. Still, there was a faint moment of hope. A fight broke out, and my friend stormed out of the room. I went after him, as I'd done lots of times before. I found him hiding between trees in the backyard, quivering and sobbing. I held him and said it was going to be okay. It was like holding a small child, trying to talk him out of the despair. Then, coming out of our clench, I said, "You need help. You've got to stop." That was the moment when he was supposed to say that he knew I was right; that he'd go back to the group and accept their offer to pay for a stay in a nearby drug and alcohol rehabilitation centre. But instead, he echoed what he'd told me years before: "You think I need help or something? You really don't think I can do this on my own?" I told him that he could not. He collected himself and returned to the meeting.

"Okay," he told us, lying down on a bed. "Tell me all of the terrible things I've done." We did. It was a positive development, because he had to hear it from us. The next day, however, someone in our group took pity on him. She told him that he could stay with her instead of going to rehab. It would be okay, she said; she'd look after him. We asked her what the fuck she was doing and she told us that she didn't think it was fair to force him to do something he didn't want to do. A few days later, he sent an email saying that he was cutting off contact with us; that he didn't want to be friends with anyone who'd tried to make him change. My friend is a grown man, and I don't know what will happen to him. You came back, Gord – you didn't even go to A.A., or do the twelve-step; you just found a doctor you liked, and you quit drinking – but I don't think everyone can. I don't know where he's headed, and sometimes I lie awake at night fearing that where he's going is a place that I don't ever want him to go.

As I write to you, I've just come back from the Vancouver Art Gallery, which is why this subject is on my mind. I was at an exhibit where a Chinese artist, Song Dong, had an installation that collected all of the things hoarded by his mother. There are countless bottles and shopping bags and fabrics and soap wrappers and other things – tons of other things – laid out on blankets, miles of stuff, pooling everywhere in the gallery, taking up three rooms. My friend was kind of a hoarder, too. I still have boxes of his stuff – tapes and newspaper magazine clippings in my basement – and in his apartment, there was junk everywhere. In any other circumstance, his room would have looked like a beautiful mess, but, instead, all of that stuff came to represent defeat, old Christmas decorations hanging off a tree past due. Touring the exhibit, I was, I think, supposed to be struck by the essence of what we leave behind – after the body is gone and the home bereft of a tenant. Dong was paying tribute to his mother's survival instincts. It's a Chinese thing, as I understand it: using whatever is at hand as a way of dealing with poverty. But with my friend, even those things were gone. But then I realized, no, at least the music is still there, still here. The body goes – or lurches towards an alcoholic abyss – but the songs stay.

Continuing to another part of the gallery, I came across a sculpture by the Korean artist Khan Lee. It was beautiful, too: a winding stack of cassette tapes stretching from floor to ceiling. My friend, of course, kept tapes, but so did I; boxes of them, documenting old recordings of band rehearsals, demos, radio shows on which we'd appeared, and albums rescued from garage sales. It wasn't until I followed the sculpture towards the top that I saw it: one of his tapes, leaning out over the gallery. I thought about my friend, about the music. I'm grateful that I can tell this to you, Gord. You don't know him and you don't know me. But now you know this sad story, and I hope it somehow helps when you read what I'm going to write next.

Before I start, someone once told me this. The person is a writer and a journalist. He lives on the west coast.

"I went to see Lightfoot play at the Place Des Arts in Montreal. I went there with a group of people who were part of a drug and addiction group, of which I was a member, trying to deal with a heroin problem. The show was great, and Lightfoot was great. He'd gotten off the drugs and the booze and looked really healthy. Somehow word reached Gord that we were there, and so he got a message to us telling us to stay after the show. So once it ended, we sat in our seats for twenty minutes as people filed out of the hall, and then Gord came out. He sat with us and talked with us – these total strangers – about our recovery for a long time. He didn't have to do it. He was just being himself and trying to support us through these times. It was a remarkable thing and I'll never forget it. You expect a lot of things from your heroes, but this, I never expected."

So, Gord, I wonder: did it start with Cathy? Or did it start before that? Reading Cathy's book, she gives the impression that you were already well into it: the booze, the sleeping around, the drugs. And you, yourself, have said, "I had a happy childhood, but the depression set in, and I've been battling it ever since." You told the press, in a moment of total honesty, "It's one of the reasons why I drink," although, in the same breath, you switched gears, boasting that "I'm a good Canadian drinker," and that, at the time, you were drinking at least a bottle a day. My friend was the same way: waffling between admissions of emotional despair and pride in his ability to maintain his habit and his lifestyle. If you were battling depression as well as addiction, I doubt that Cathy was helpful in the way of therapy. Instead, you found an abusive twin, with bouts of passion thrown in there to sustain interest in each other. I'm not telling you anything that you don't know, but you weren't the first artist, and you won't be the last, to find someone willing to support whatever kind of lifestyle you choose. Acolytes – groupies, fan kids, partiers – are the worst kind of enablers, in a way. They'll stroke you when you're lying face-down in your own puke. They're not outraged or offended or disappointed when you say the worst possible things to them.

Cathy had already been with Richard Manuel and had given birth to Levon's kid, Tracey Lee, whom she'd given up, just as she'd been given up herself. To you, she provided a kind of physical poetry, not to mention providing drugs and a place to hide. In her, you could lay your insecurities, fears, and your gathering sense of darkness and mortality. She both normalized the rock and roll life while pushing it into a fast and delicious orbit. She'd let you do whatever you wanted. She was a dark angel who comforted you because she understood how fucked up and impossible it was to live this kind of life. She knew that you thought you were a fraud – that every successful artist feels like a fraud, living the kind of life that most people can only dream of – and that you feared that your success would soon be devoured, and that God would one day steal from you the good fortune and luck that had sustained your career while others were back home selling insurance or playing in cover bands.

At home, you had to suppress these fears. We all did. We didn't want to drag our shit into our loved ones' lives. That's why gigging was so important, and why the parties were, too. Still, while Cathy writes about how fucked up things were, she also writes about the shows, and how you could do whatever you wanted with your music. You had absolute control over your songs even though, at the time, your life was spinning away from you.

Everybody talks about the theatre shows. They talk about how you used to sweep your hand over your instrument's body and how the notes would fall as if they were the feathers of a soft shedding beast; chords like butterscotch, your voice like hard candy. Back then, it was okay to appear gentle and poised on stage, one finger on the mercury catch of a long glass thermometer, controlling the room's collective heat. It wasn't about immediate detonation: a cheap clowning burst of incendiary surprise that leaves the room with nothing but stale smoke. Back then, in the halls and velvet theatres, you'd slipper to your spot beside a stool that held a water jug and a few sheaves of lyrics, pausing to draw in the expectations and uncertainties of the crowd, utter a few disarming words, and, slowly, carefully, show them your quiet power, and whatever might explode would explode from within: an emotional rupture, a fissure of release in the darkened chamber that held what needed to be freed. Some nights, not a single drop was produced. Some nights, the bastards sat there incapable of release, but thank God you were travelling. Thank God you weren't so stubborn that you bled any more than you had to for the ungrateful saps in Canton, Ohio, or Madison, Wisconsin, or Albany, New York, who sat expressionless in places named The Smirking Parrot or Uncle Joe's Roadside Dive or Che's, and gave back nothing.

After shows, there were hotel rooms; countless hotel rooms. When we toured, it was always a crappy Sandman Inn, although you probably stayed in better places. Still, you'd go to your hotel room: brown drapes, an airbrushed painting of any town other than the one you were in riveted above the headboard, two water glasses upturned on the wooden nightstand, and the crumbs of the previous night's travelling shower-ring salesman seeding the edges of the wall where he'd eaten a packet of crackers while masturbating to Barbi Benton being interviewed by Mike Douglas on a shitty TV that shook when you thumbed the ON button harder than you had to.

Sometimes, you had a friend, even though you had Cathy, and, for a time, Brit, waiting at home. During the show, she'd been sitting close to the stage fucking you with her eyes while you played or sometimes she appeared out of the club's shadows, a brunette with a leather shoulder bag. Sometimes she followed you back to your room because someone else she'd been with had stayed in the same hotel the week before and sometimes you cared that she'd been with him but most times you did not, because if it was purity you were looking for you were in the wrong game. Sometimes she was charcoal-drawn wearing mostly black with boots up to her asscheeks and sometimes she was the mayor's daughter straight out of high school wanting to drink from the poisoned well of adult-hood. Sometimes they came because they were curious about how you put together your songs and sometimes they wanted your dick as a trophy and sometimes they thought they could show you something that was wilder than what you'd seen on tour, which, if you'd just swung through the American midwest or Thunder Bay, it probably was not. Sometimes they'd want to hold your hand for awhile or talk about books or discuss politics, and sometimes they couldn't wait to crack open the booze and tear off their clothes and hit the bed or carpet busy and fast. Sometimes they'd say "Nice room," or "Hey, can I see your guitar?" or "Do you want to have a shower?" or, in your case, maybe they said, "You know, I orgasmed the first time I heard 'If You Could Read My Mind.'" Sometimes, they'd want to talk before sex, and sometimes they'd want to talk after. Sometimes they wanted the lights on and sometimes they wanted them off and sometimes they brought their own things, like ropes or handcuffs or vibrators or Polaroid cameras or creams or oils or, once, a purse with these little cables and an electric box which you plugged in before fastening them to her nipples, which is actually something that happened to another musician I know. Sometimes they cried afterwards and sobbed, "How could I do this to him?" and sometimes they wanted to stay and sometimes they asked for your shirt as a souvenir and sometimes they told you about what the bass player from a lesser band was like and sometimes they wanted you to meet their parents and sometimes they just got dressed and got the fuck out, which, sometimes, you preferred.

Gale Zoe Garnett told me about sleeping with you. In San Francisco, after her band, Gale Garnett and the Gentle Reign, opened for you. I didn't go around looking for people you'd slept with, Gord. I don't care, not really. Gale is a very open and honest person, and when we were talking, she just said it. She told me, "The following morning I gave him a necklace of olive green Peking beads. He told me, 'I've been here (in San Francisco) for a few days, and no one has given me beads.' He seemed kind of hurt by it, so I gave him mine. Gord was a very straight Scottish Presbyterian guy. He wasn't putting me on. He was very touched by it. He was, in a way, a terrific inno-cent. I think that he was always looking for Laura Secord in the middle of a dirty movie, searching for that purity somehow. Bobby Neuwirth, Dylan's friend, had been with us earlier and he was a very toxic presence. He said, 'You just want to blow him.' I told him, 'No way! I'm not even good at that.' To be honest, everyone was drunk, and I didn't think that it was the best thing for Gord to climb into a vehicle at that point. It was very sweet, very innocent. It was the sixties, sure, but it didn't feel like it that night, not once we were alone."

Another woman told me stuff, then another, then another. They weren't hard to find, Gord. Some were less forgiving than others. One of them told me that you gave her what you considered to be the highest compliment possible. You compared her to "my true love, Cathy." Another said that you wanted "something wild one last time." Finally, another told me: "I loved the artist and liked the sad man. Though were he just a man, I wouldn't have done it."

Drugs and booze go with sex the way the rain follows a billowing mass of storm clouds. Nineteen seventy through 1972 was bad. In her chapter called (obviously) "That's What You Get for Loving Me," Cathy says that you were stoned on pills when you hung her upside down from a twenty-first storey balcony in Hawaii. A security guard started pounding on the door, and he talked you out of dropping her. Cathy says that, one time, you pushed her head into the toilet. Confronted with this accusation, you told Maynard Collins: "It was a clean toilet bowl. If there was anything in it, I absolutely would have not done that." Cathy says that you hit her, too, breaking her cheekbone with one punch. She needed plastic surgery, which you paid for. Cathy hit back, too, of course, and, soon, it was all just a terrible shitfest of pain and hatred. It was *The Days of Wine and Roses* all over again: two people who'd become horrible within themselves, to themselves, and to each other.

Still, Cathy bounced back rubbery and free even after the worst times. And then you'd go back to your band to continue working on the greatest body of Canadian songs ever conceived. What the fuck? Excuse the fans — at least some of us — for seeing you as some kind of heroic party monster, with the ability to write great songs while completely out of your head.

I don't know Cathy Evelyn Smith, although I've tried looking for her. She was busted a few years ago for junk in Vancouver's East Side, and that's the last anyone heard of her. Maybe she could put some of the pieces together, but maybe not. To draw a portrait, I asked my friend, Trevor Weeks, the photographer, to fill me in. His mom grew up with Cathy. This is what he said:

"Cathy is a fascinating person. I know of her because my mother was her best friend from early childhood into high school. They lived across the road from each other on Shadeland Avenue in Burlington for most of their lives until high school. Around that point, in their teenage years, they drifted apart as they were becoming two different people. My mom was a good girl, and Cathy was a little more rough around the edges. My mom met my dad after high school and they moved to England for a couple years to study and teach. Sometime after they returned, they both ran into Mrs. Smith (Cathy's mum) at a grocery store. My mom introduced Mrs. Smith to my dad, and Mrs. Smith pulled a photo of Cathy from her purse. She said that Cathy had moved to Toronto and was living with a musician. My parents were folkies and recognized Cathy's boyfriend in the photo right away. Mrs. Smith said his name was Gordon and he was trying to make it as a musician. Later on, they found themselves in Toronto one day and decided to look her up to say hello. It turned out that Cathy was pretty spaced out. They had nothing in common because my parents never did drugs, and Cathy was clearly somewhere else. They never saw her again."

There are times in Cathy's book when she describes sleeping with you in the beginning, and her memories seem, I dunno, kind of sweet. She describes the late night clandestine rendezvous in her apartment that leave her – and you, apparently – feeling like kids sneaking off to neck behind the portables. But things got bad fast, foreshadowing your portrait of her in "Sundown," which, if it wasn't such a well-crafted country rock song, would be regarded as one of the toughest and maybe meanest sets of lyrics ever written about anyone. It would be regarded as plainly misogynistic, I think, if the narrator – the narrator being you – didn't come across like such a mess. But even if you didn't hang her out the window, your relationship started to blacken. You did terrible things to your girlfriend, and she did terrible things to you.

You lived with Cathy in a high-rise apartment called Tower on the Village Green. Actually, you kept an apartment, because you were still officially married to Brita. While Toronto is now walled with high rises and elite condominiums, back then living above the city would have been a privilege, a stripe of achievement. You would have shared your building with well-heeled magazine publishers, Bay Street lawyers, radio personalities, and monied Irish and Scots from old Orange Toronto, its lobby fitted with a painting by Harold Town, decorated in Art Shoppe chic. You would have been distanced from the streetcar's roar, or the stench of Chinatown. You were part of the new Toronto, seventies Toronto. But despite the sense of status this conferred, you couldn't escape your roots. Like Bernie Finkelstein told me: "Gordon was always the small-town guy no matter where he went. I think that came out in a lot of his parties. He was always getting into it with somebody or other, whatever the occasion."

Collins gives us a clear picture of the apartment. Quoting Cathy, he writes that "it was a total bachelor fantasy," and that it had "deep-piled rugs and a spring-loaded top to the coffee table to hide the marijuana stash. The apartment's decor ran to red-flecked wallpaper, deep gold velvet couches . . . Tiffany lamps, Eskimo carvings and paintings on the wall, including a (Robert) Markle portrait." He says that, during the early seventies, you were "a perplexed and worried man," and that, during a canoe trip, you decided to try and make your life with Brita work. It didn't. You went back to Cathy, found out that she'd screwed around, and called her a slut. You threw her out of the apartment (the two of you would reconnect, of course) and so she hitchhiked down to San Francisco to see The Good Brothers. Collins makes another point, too. Apparently, your album, *Back Here On Earth,* was falling below sales expectations. It was the first time there was a lag in momentum since you started making hit records. And, as Tom Hopkins writes in his *Maclean's* story, "though he has the upper body of a stevedore, hardened by canoeing and running sailboats, he has the lower body of a beer parlour waiter. His face is as bloodless and distended as half-risen bread dough. He repeatedly tips a bottle of C.C. rye into a plastic cup of coffee, continuing to top it up until the coffee is gone." All of these issues weighed on you as you slouched towards 1972.

Because you shouldn't read Cathy's book, I'll tell you a story that's in it, and who knows if it's true. But it's in there. It's strange story, and sad. In a way, it brings it all back to Dylan. The story goes like this:

You and Cathy were in that break-up-one-minute-but-get-back-together-the-next period. In this instance, you guys were apart. You'd argued and Cathy had split. The Band and Dylan were in town and they were staying at the Inn on the Park. Apparently, they'd rented a few floors of the hotel for themselves. Cathy decided to go see them with her friend Sally, and somehow, you found out. It made you jealous, and so you followed them. You drove at night along the highway to the city's northeast corner and who knows what you were expecting to find or why you even went there in the first place. Once you were at the hotel, you skulked around. You followed the couple as they rode the elevator to where the musicians were staying. One image in particular stayed with me, which I think, defines what you were feeling at this time in your life: suspicious, alone, confused, drunk, angry, stoned, and hurt. She writes:

"As Sally and I travelled up and down the elevator, I was aware that Gordon was hot on my trail. I was standing against the wall while the doors closed, and, through the mirror, I could see Gordon (sneaking around) and getting off the other elevator, wringing his hands as though he wished my neck were between them."

I don't know if you still think about Cathy or the things that happened during those times. You've told people that you can't – or won't – write a book because you don't want to go back to the memories of that life. You want to stay as far away as possible from Cathy, which is good, because you've come through the other side, and going back there at your age would probably be a bad idea. Cathy was once the centre of your life – a terrible dark life – but, growing old, you've protected yourself from ever going back there. So don't.

Dan Hill dated Cathy right after you. His experiences weren't quite as incendiary, but it was no joyride, either. Once, Cathy demanded that Dan accompany her to a party thrown in honour of Joni Mitchell in Laurel Canyon. Dan remembers: "There were all of these L.A. Rams football players there; huge guys with bulging crotches. It was as though some woman – I suspect Joni, but that's just a hunch – designed the party as a kind of Hugh Hefner thing in reverse, from a woman's point of view. It was fascinating, in a way, even though I felt totally out of place with all of these L.A. pretentious hot shots and poseurs, people who wouldn't look at you unless you were somebody. I was twenty-two. I had a chip on my shoulder, but still. And then she went upstairs with this famous Hollywood actor and started fucking him, abandoning me at the party. I ended up running back to the Hyatt. I was mad at her and didn't talk to her for a year; not because she'd fucked this Hollywood actor, but because she'd brought me all the way out there only to abandon me at the party surrounded by creeps. I saw her a year later at that same Hyatt, and ended up going back to my room with her. It was a Sunday. When we got there, she started emptying this stuff on the top of my set. I asked her what it was and she said, "It's heroin." It was her way of making it up to me for going upstairs with the actor. She always used to call me a wimp, but I said, 'You're right, Cathy. I'm a Don Mills wimp, but there ain't no way I'm snorting heroin off the top of a TV set.' This was 1979, just before John Belushi died.

"In her defence – and maybe mine – Cathy was beautiful, charismatic, and smart," said Dan. "I was at a stage in my life when I was drawn to the bad girl, and maybe she had the same allure for Gord. I hadn't had a very exciting life in terms of adventure, and while there was an alert danger about her, there was seductive quality to it, too, more so when you're young and just getting established in the music industry. Her job was the everything woman. She'd take your kids to school, go shopping, do your books because she was bright, and then she'd fuck you. In the music business, that wasn't thought of as strange at all."

I wonder where Cathy is. Or if she's even alive. Since you won't talk to me, maybe she will. But if it means queering the deal between you and me – and by the way, is there a deal; do we have one yet? – then, no, I won't look for her.

I

am

out.

THE END OF THE WEEKEND

S uch were the circumstances of Mariposa '72 that no sooner had Bob Dylan left then Neil Young appeared. True to form, he drifted wraith-like through the scene, arriving on the island unnoticed. In the middle of Dylanmania, his presence wasn't felt as deeply, nor was it as great an organizational millstone. Neil mostly hung out in the tent with his new wife Carrie Snodgress, keeping to himself. Snodgress was six months pregnant, and, in September, she gave birth to Neil's first son, Zeke. Bruce Cockburn ended up sharing his set time with Young, which made him feel, he said, "somewhat mildly resentful." The twenty-six-year-old songwriter, who'd just finished touring his number one album, *Harvest,* played four songs solo on acoustic guitar: "Helpless," "Heart of Gold," "Sugar Mountain," and "Harvest." While it isn't clear why he came to Mariposa, he wasn't unconnected to the festival. Bob Young, Neil's brother, was a festival volunteer as well as

Neil Young at Mariposa, 1972

journalist for Goddard's *Touch* magazine, so it's possible that he was visiting him. It's also possible that Neil was drawn to the festival through Bernie Finkelstein's partner, Bernie Fiedler, who ran the Riverboat, where both Neil and Joni cut their teeth in the mid-sixties. Dan Hill said that, "except for

Dylan, all of the Mariposa guests had played the Riverboat, and they had a fondness for Fiedler, going back to before they were famous. Jackson Browne used to play there all of the time. After shows, he'd stay through the night and write. Also, Toronto, at the time, was the perfect place for everyone to meet. It was a great folksinger's city, and there were less than a half dozen of those in America." Michael Cooney suggested another reason why these musicians came together at Mariposa: "At any given moment, all of the molecules in the air can rush to one side of the room. The odds are against it, but it's possible. Maybe that's the only way to explain what happened on the island."

It's also possible that, in Neil's case, the island environs and tone of the event were the right kind of musical balm for the emerging superstar, who, in short time, would find himself disenchanted with the life of a best-selling artist. Very little about what happened during his set could have portended the musical — and emotional — shift that was about to envelop his career. In fact, Neil's turn at Mariposa would be one of the last pure moments of unaffected balladry before the songwriter pushed his repertoire face first into the ditch, ignoring the demands of conventional hit-making. His next tour would feature mostly new songs sung through a haze of alcohol abuse and mental instability, and, a year later, he'd exile "Heart of Gold" from his set. The golden honey of his Southern California-by-way-of-Winnipeg sound would roll over for songs with chords that growled out of shitty amps and a band — the Stray Gators — who pushed his music slurving towards the rock and roll abyss of his subsequent excellent records: *Time Fades Away, On the Beach,* and *Tonight's the Night.* No musician would more closely shadow the crooked path of what was to become of the decade, his music growing more poignant as the seventies lurched toward North American economic decline, pornography, hostage peril, fast food, slums, and bad drugs. Mariposa '72 was the last time Neil Young would allow his art to bathe in providence under the softness of the sun. It was a subtle gift to the fans, their city and their scene, one final gesture before gutting his sound from the inside out, and getting a jump on the emerging forces that would make peace and love their bitch.

There was another thing that happened during Neil's set. You probably know what I'm talking about, Gord, although maybe you don't. Maybe – like the Mariposa volunteers – your memory is a little jumbled. Maybe you can remember what it was like to be on the island with your friend, Dylan, and how, after all of the craziness had settled down and the crowd was about to head back to the city and that kid with the twisted face and stringy hair was finishing his set, you came out from the backstage area, walked over to a narrow stand of trees and thought: ah, fuck it. You grabbed a guitar and sat down. You started playing.

Maybe you did this as an act of solace. Maybe you did it as a way of getting yourself – or the festival or folk music; I dunno – back to its essence. Or maybe you were just trying to steady things for a moment because 1972 was a crazy year for you, just as it was a crazy year for the country, too, and a crazy year for the world. That's one of the reasons why I wanted to write this book, Gord: to look at the year – well, actually, the week; a year in a week – and how it affected people's lives, their world, and their culture, especially in Canada. If you've read this book, you probably know all of the things that happened in that week. Maybe you learned things you didn't know because, at the time, you were busy dealing with your own shit: the palsy and its weird medication, the drinking, Cathy Evelyn, your collapsed marriage, and your career. Still, because I don't know if you've read it, I'll explain a few things in case you just flipped through most of the book to the last chapter wanting to see how things turned out in the end. That's a joke. Sorry.

Okay. So all of these things happened that week, and, on the weekend, they continued happening. On Sunday, just as you and Bob and Neil and Joni were coming together, a spacecraft – Pioneer 10 – passed unblemished through the asteroid belt. I don't want to come across as being trippy, Gord, but I believe that stuff like this – stuff like the penetration of the solar system – matters to the earth, being an important member of that system and everything. The event happened far away, but people must have sensed it: an imperceptible wave that rippled across the sky. Not only that, but it happened almost a week to the day after the total eclipse of the sun, the one that Carly Simon wrote about in "You're So Vain." I wonder whether what was happening in the sky made you sit down by yourself to play even though there was no stage, no mics, or no lighting, because, from what people tell me, you are very particular about that sort of thing. Hundreds of miles away, Pioneer 10's conquest was announced in a few flickers of light that passed across a pixelated screen at NASA command control in Houston. The white-shirted men who worked there were beside themselves when they saw the exotic orange-ice-cream glow of Jupiter on the screen. They jumped and hollered and grabbed each other by the hands and shoulders. They shouted that it was a great day for America, a great day for humanity. This generation of technicians would give way to another before, in 2003, contact with the spacecraft would disappear entirely. But in that exultant moment, man had proven that he could reach beyond himself, that he could defy expectations. It wasn't time for coffee, Gord. No way. The men celebrated. They drank champagne. And smoked fine cigars from anywhere but Cuba.

Another thing happened on Sunday, Gord, which reminds me: do you like chess? Did you and Whelan ever play it when you were kids? Do you play it with your grandkids? What happened was that the Icelandic governing committee of the Spassky–Fischer chess summit finally received the Russian federation's shot across the bow, a tersely-worded letter of protest. Organizers were relieved, Gord. There was no threat of walking away from the match; none of the intellectual or emotional stonewalling that had come from Fischer and the Americans. Instead, the Soviets had acted with a relative grace that, in the end, cost them the game, the match, and the world championship of chess. On Sunday, Fischer ended up ambushing a weakened Spassky. He used his savvy and intellect to disassemble the Russian, and then, almost instantly, he disappeared from public, not playing again competitively until twenty years later. Nothing was gained from his victory other than victory itself, Gord, and a once-estimable pastime was plunged into sporting darkness. Similarly, while Canada's victory over Team Russia will be remembered for its dramatic national mood swings and wild scores – I know you remember this event, Gord, being a hockey fan and everything – it was only a year later that the game descended into a terrible decade of stick swinging and long-haired brawling: violence raging in the white light of the arena that welcomed only those who could fight as well as they could score, sometimes more so. It wasn't until the end of the seventies – 1980 – that Wayne Gretzky rescued the game from itself. He wore a JOFA helmet and played more like a Russian than any player who'd come before him. Really, the only constant between then and now is that the Leafs still suck. Gord, I put that in there in case you happen to be reading.

So with all of these things happening, you sat down and you started playing. I talked to people who were there and who watched you. Bradley Harding recalls: "Lightfoot was sitting by a big tree with the Good Brothers. There was almost no one around at first, and then I remember one of the Goods saying, 'Hey, look everybody, it's Gordon Lightfoot and the Good Brothers!'" Tex McLeod remembered: "On Sunday, I turned a corner thinking that I could see Gordon Lightfoot sitting on the grass under a tree playing to a few people. I gave my head a shake, but as I got closer, I saw that it was him.

There was no security, nothing like that." Leigh Cline said: "Gordon Lightfoot did things the right way. He just took out his guitar and played. He never asked to be part of some actual performance. Sitting under a tree and playing for a few dozen people was his performance." And then Ken Whiteley told me: "I remember coming across Lightfoot, playing with the Goods. Someone had a banjo out and Gord had a guitar and they just started. Because they were in a spot removed from where the stages were, there were only about thirty or forty people around. I'm sure a lot of people passed by and thought, 'Oh, there's another guy who thinks he's Gordon Lightfoot.' But it was simple and very sweet. It was one of those moments that Mariposa, at its best, was all about."

After that weekend, you came back and you came back strong. You kept having hit records, Gord. "Sundown" was about to be born. So was "The Wreck of the Edmund Fitzgerald," and did I tell you? Just as I was finishing this book, I played that song at the Horseshoe as part of this seventies Juno night with our old bass player, Tim, singing the song, doing it together for the first time in at least a decade. Loads of other people did your songs, too. It's 2011 and people are still playing your songs, Gord; playing them hard, with a lot of passion. The Good Brothers played at the Horseshoe, too. Ironic, right? There were rumours that you were going to come to the show, but you never did (not like at friggin' Hugh's Room. *Argggh*). But that's okay. We played "The Wreck of the Edmund Fitzgerald." We ripped it up. Our guitarist made whale sounds and the band rocked. It was probably the best we'd done it since the time we did it at Cobo Hall, which I've written about before – did I tell you? I have nine other books, Gord; some about rock and roll, but some about hockey, which I think you'd like, but maybe that's just me – but even though I've written about it before, I want to tell you what it was like that night in Cobo Hall.

We were opening for the Tragically Hip. I know you know them because, in 2009, you did a concert – well sort of an interview-concert – with Gord Downie. I hear it was great, but I couldn't go. Anyway, that afternoon in Detroit, as soon as soundcheck ended, Tim, the song's singer, went for a walk to find the Maritime Sailor's Museum, the same one that you sing about in the song. Because we were opening the night, we hadn't planned on playing the song. We had limited stage-time that tour, so we stuffed our set with shorter songs. When Tim got back, he asked if I thought we should play it, and I said that we definitely should, even though it would take up about one quarter of our set. So we did. It was our last song. When it ended, people stood up in the crowd and cheered. It would be the only time that would happen all tour, and the only time we would play the song.

At the Horseshoe, Dan Hill also played. We did "Sometimes When We Touch" with him, and it ended the night. It was spectacular. Everyone was singing along and going crazy and you could feel the floor being lifted off the ground. A few days later, Dan told me a story about you and Tim Hardin. It's also about you and Dan. It goes like this:

"Gord was good to a lot of musicians. Tim Hardin stayed with him just before he died, and he was going through terrible methadone withdrawal. Gord was quite concerned and so, one time, when it was particularly bad, Gord asked, 'Can I go out and get you some aspirin or something?' Hardin looked at him like he was crazy. But Gord was just trying to help.

"I never saw the mean or angry side of Gord, even though, you know, I'd heard stories. He was always sweet to me. In 1977, I was having really bad girlfriend problems. She told me that she never wanted to see me again and she kicked me out. I'd been in love with her since I was fifteen years old. I'd finished a show in Moncton and I figured that the only chance I had to reconcile with her was going to happen that night if it happened at all, but I had a show in St. John, N.B., the following day. Bernie Fiedler said 'Let's call Lightfoot and see if we can borrow his Lear Jet.' Gord told me, 'Ya, I can get you this jet on five thousand dollars credit, and I'll front you the money.' It was such a generous thing to do. After I thanked him, he said, 'But I'll tell you right now, there ain't no woman in the world who's worth five thousand dollars.' It was such a perfect Lightfoot quote. I'll never forget this Lear jet coming into Moncton airport at two in the morning. Gord had just come through his huge divorce, so he might have been extra sympathetic, I don't know." In his book, Collins wrote that when Brita's lawyer left the courtroom, he was humming one of your songs, "That's What You Get For Lovin' Me."

Dan wanted to put this story in his excellent memoir, *I Am My Father's Son,* but the lawyers – or I guess the publisher's lawyers – told him not to. Maybe the lawyers will be right about this book. Maybe I shouldn't have written it. But I can't stop here, and besides, there's something else. It might piss you off more, provided you are pissed off, which I hope you're not, though you probably are. Still, it's something that I thought of after being out at the Olympics last winter. I know you were at the Calgary Olympics – you played the Opening Ceremonies – and I know that you did benefits for the Montreal Olympics in 1976. But no, you weren't in Vancouver. You weren't there because you were at home in Toronto. I know this – we all know this – because, just after the Olympics started, I got an email from Stephen Brunt, the writer, who is a big fan of yours. A long time ago, he wanted to write a book about you, but he wrote about Bobby Orr instead, who wouldn't talk to him, either. The book became a big, big seller, and there's that connection again. Orr, Lightfoot, Canada. Right there.

Anyhow, he emailed to tell me that you were dead, or, at least, that there were reports all over his *Globe and Mail* newsroom that you had died. You'd just come through some terrible health problems – a stomach aneurysm that led to a stroke – so the news wasn't surprising, though, of course, it was sad and affecting. Still, in a way, I thought it would be a weirdly appropriate time for you to check out. The reason I say this (and I feel morbid even writing it, but bear with me) is because all that you'd started back in the sixties – articulating the Canadian experience and summoning the right kind of pride from the right kind of sources – was on display those two weeks in February in Vancouver. Gord, you wouldn't have believed it. Groups of men and women, kids and grandparents, marched through the city singing "O Canada," and even when

Canada wasn't winning over the first few days, there was a huge feeling of self-determination, empowerment, pride, and joy. It was astonishing. The wave rippled and rippled and got huge. It consumed the city; it consumed the country. And it was all because you – you and maybe Trudeau – hucked the first pebble in the pond. But you weren't in Vancouver. You were at home and you were dead. Only you weren't dead. Not yet. But I don't have to tell you that.

The press called Ronnie Hawkins and he said, "Yup, Gord's dead," or something like that. But then someone actually got a hold of you, and you told them that, nope, you weren't dead, even though, for a few hours, all that anyone talked about on the streets of Vancouver and in the cafes, garages, and kitchens of the country was that Canada's greatest living songwriter was gone. Word of the Games; of Canada's fortunes in them; of the tragic death of the Georgian luger; of the IOC; of Team Canada: all of that stopped. The nation stilled and, for a moment, it mourned.

Here's what I think, and, Gord, try to not get mad. I think you faked it. You or someone you know. I think you were sitting back watching it all go down – watching the Opening Ceremonies with these other musicians, k.d. lang and Neil Young, getting a chance to play – and you thought, in a moment of mischief, that you would try and bring the nation's thoughts back to the source: back to you. It's a crazy theory, yeah, I know. It's probably ridiculous. But that's what I think. Maybe, during that event, the country needed to remember that which had helped produce all of this pride and enthusiasm. You. It stemmed from you; a great folksinger and primo mischievous son of a bitch.

Gord, this book is almost over. And with its conclusion, I have another confession to make. The confession is this: I am full of shit. I am so totally full of shit because just as I was finishing this book, something happened. It came to me, it found me. It was information. I kept it in my pocket like a stolen jewel, even though I hadn't stolen it. Sometimes information is the worst thing to possess. But once I possessed it, I knew that I had to use it, even though I didn't want to.

It's not bad information, not really. But maybe it's revealing information, I don't know. I told you that, after I announced my intentions to write this book, people told me to steer clear of you. They said that you were a miserable and vindictive bastard and that I was only asking for trouble. And the lawyers – man, the lawyers didn't want any part of this. But like I said, to hell with lawyers. I don't give a fuck. I was given the ability to write a little – heck, not even the ability; but the zeal, the energy, the passion, the joy – and because it's what I do, it's also what I have to do. So I wrote. I wrote and wrote and wrote. About you. You're not the only one. I've written about lots of other people, but this time, I've written about you. And as I began this book, I realized that your detractors weren't right, not entirely. Over the course of this writing, I started to hear some really cool stories, ones that flattered you. My idea of you as a person started to change. And this made me decide to use this information, rather than keep it tucked in the darkness of my coat pocket, or whatever metaphor you want to use for the place where one harbours things that they think about but don't write, at least not in a book that will, hopefully, get read by people, lots of people, who will understand what I'm writing about. Still, what makes this information difficult is that the person who gave it to me asked not to be quoted, further confusing matters, at least for me. In this book, I didn't want to get anybody in trouble, especially not you, Gord. And I don't want to get the person who gave me the information in trouble, either.

A lot of biographies have been written where the author unearths something new about their subject. It usually involves some deep secret that incriminates the subject, or exposes them in a negative way. The thing with my bit of information is that – although it is secret – it works the other way. I think it actually exposes you as a good guy, touching on some of the sentiments expressed earlier in the book, about you being generous and helpful and all of that. So I feel less bad writing it, even though I don't know how it will affect you or your family or your legacy or our relationship, which we don't have, but which I'd like to have someday. But you know that already.

The information is about you and Cathy Smith. When I asked someone who knows you whether or not you guys stay in contact, he told me, "No way. Gord is trying to put that part of his past to rest." Someone else told me that one of the reasons you didn't want to have any part of this book – or any book – was because you couldn't handle being once again associated with Cathy, or what she represented in terms of your life and legacy and reputation.

But I know that you're still in touch with her. I know that you help her out and that you support her. I know that you send her money and that, even though every other celebrity or famous person with whom she's crossed paths wants nothing to do with her — not Levon, not the Stones, not the Saturday Night Live crew nor Jack Nicholson nor Warren Beatty — it isn't the case with you because you care. I know that Cathy is living in Ontario and that even though you've moved on to build a clean and good life playing seventy shows a year at seventy-two years of age, the past still tugs at you and you still tug at the past. I don't know how all of this came to be. I don't know whether you went looking for her or she went looking for you, or whether — after years trying to outrun the ghosts of your personal life — you decided to let her find you, and then deal with whatever consequences followed. Most people want their ghosts to disappear, and it's how I thought it was with you. But this ghost, you kept close. You kept it alive.

You won't talk about Cathy Smith. Not in interviews, not anywhere. But knowing that you are still in contact with her makes me think that, through all of the darkness and depression and regret and anxiety and worries and troubles, something like a kind of peace or reckoning has found its way into your life, to say nothing of the guy-handing-out-candy-on-Halloween contentment that appears to have come with being sober and straight-minded in your seventh decade. Before, it was always either the music that defined your greatness, or the persona which, for some people, cancelled out your

Cathy Smith and Gord

greatness. But now, it's almost reversed. You haven't had a hit record for decades, yet you show up for charity auctions in small towns to play "Black Day in July" or call superfans like Char Westbrook — she writes about you, posts pictures of you on the Internet, runs websites and forums devoted to you — to wish them happy birthday. Sylvia Tyson once told me: "Gordon is much more open than before. Much more gregarious. He used to be very self-contained, very driven. But now it seems as if he's finally enjoying the fruits of his labours. There was a time when all he wanted was to be in the mainstream of pop music, but that's not an issue anymore. I'm glad that I know Gordon at this stage in his life. A lot of people are."

So, the sonofabitch is reborn. A good phoenix. Not only

are you apparently not a bastard anymore, but look, you gave the writer who wrote about you an ending for his book.

I feel okay having written this. I wonder how you feel. There's an exhilaration that comes with ending a book, and maybe you're feeling a kind of exhilaration, too, having come to what is not quite the end of your career, your legacy, your life. Maybe you're exhilarated, too – or maybe you're relieved – because there are probably lots of other things that I could have put in this book, but did not. Maybe a more intense biographer – or, sure, maybe a better biographer – would have included them, but I didn't. I don't know. I'm sure that as soon as this book comes out, I'll hear other stories. You always hear other stories. Some of them I'll regret not having heard before finishing this book. It's the way it always is. One time, after writing about another musician, someone asked me: "Did he tell you the story about what happened in Miami in '76?" He hadn't. After hearing the story, I was glad that he hadn't told me. Although it would have made for a better biography, it wouldn't have made for a better book. Do you know what I mean? It would have sold more. It would have made more money. For me. It would have gotten more reaction from an increasingly voyeuristic public. It would have been more sensational. Miami '76. Do you get it? Do you understand the choices I made while writing this book? Have you been listening to anything I've said? Are you there? Are you even fucking there?

Sorry. Sometimes this kind of shit just pours out, being so close to the end. It's my last chance to express what's inside me. My last verse. You understand. I'm sure you understand.

Way back in the beginning, what got me interested in writing this book was what I'd heard about you playing at Mariposa, at a picnic table, with your friends, in front of a handful of people, just playing. I didn't know anything about Cathy or the drugs or depression. All I knew were the songs. And, in the end, it's what this book is about. It's about the playing. The songs. Winter. Radio. Canada. Words. Concerts. Mariposa. And lots of pretty Canadian chicks.

After what happened on Sunday at Mariposa, when four of the world's greatest songwriters collected on a small island at the bottom of my city – your city, our city – you kept on drinking and doing all of the other stuff you did. There were ups and downs, but years later, you pulled yourself out of it. Things were simple in that one moment on the island. You drew your guitar from your case, grabbed a pick from someone. Cathy Evelyn was there, standing behind you. It was shady and cool under the trees, and people started to gather quietly, not in the maniac way they were going after Dylan. You swigged on a beer and you looked across the field. You cleared your throat and put your hand on the fretboard. You were at home and the grass was soft to the touch.

ACKNOWLEDGEMENTS

There is lots of made-up stuff in this book. What's not made up are the stories that people told me about Mariposa '72, and without them, there would be no book. So: thanks. I'd also like to thank my family, band, and friends; Toronto libraries, which is where I did most of my writing; Tourism Ontario; the *National Post* and Ben Errett; my agent, Samantha Haywood of TLA; Doug Pepper at M&S (who rescued this book from publishing oblivion); Art Usherson for his beautiful photographs; Janet Morassutti, who copy-edited the book; Linda Pruessen, who proofread it; and my hard-working and tolerant editor, Jane Warren, who originally acquired *WGL* for Key Porter, but was kept on as it shuttled between houses. I would also like to thank Gordon Lightfoot, although it might be more practical for me to ask you to thank Gordon for me, should you see him anytime soon.